PRAISE FOR
THE SH!T NO ONE TELLS YOU

Named one of "3 Must-Have Books on Parenting" by *Fit Pregnancy*

Named one of "27 Baby Gifts That'll Make
New Parents LOL" by PopSugar

Named one of the "Best Parenting Books That Are
Definitely Worth a Read" by *Woman's Day*

"Humorous revelations offer insight into a natural process that can and often does completely overwhelm the mother.... An amusing and accurate examination of life with an infant."

—*Kirkus*

"Babies are wonderful—we all agree. Can we also acknowledge that bringing home that first bundle of joy is one of the hardest things you'll ever do? Dawn Dais bravely goes where other baby books don't in her wisecracking new release called *The Sh!t No One Tells You*. She spills the truth about everything from breastfeeding to getting along with your partner post-baby. Pregnant women who want an honest peek inside what's to come will be convinced to nap while they still can, and moms with kids will laugh out loud at Dais's quirky insights and strong opinions."

—*Parents*

"From poop to post-partum depression, Dais presents a no-holds-barred look at all of the changes and challenges that new moms and dads can face, along with the three little words every infant-toting parent wants to hear: it gets better."

—*Parade*

"Having a baby is magical, amazing, and beautiful. It's also super hard and sometimes (especially on sleepless nights) a seemingly impossible challenge. As the title, uh, delicately puts it, this book covers all the sh!t that no one tells you so you can actually survive your baby's first blissful/crazy year."

—*Woman's Day*

"Laugh-out-loud funny and filled with fantastic, first-hand advice, *The Sh!t No One Tells You* is essential reading for any new mom."

—Andrea Owen, author of *How to Stop Feeling Like Sh*t*

"Dais and her team of MOFLs (moms on the front lines) guide parents (moms, especially) through the first fifty-two weeks of your child's life with honesty, clarity, humor, complaints, and encouragement."

—Kirsten Ott Palladino, EquallyFamily.com

"*The Sh!t No One Tells You* took me right back to those first weeks of new motherhood—truly the most empowering and frustrating (and frightening!) of times. With heartfelt encouragement and insight, Dawn Dais is a must-read for first-time moms."

—Rebecca Woolf, author of *Rockabye: From Wild to Child*

THE SH!T
NO ONE TELLS YOU

THE SH!T

NO ONE TELLS YOU

A GUIDE TO SURVIVING
YOUR BABY'S FIRST YEAR

Revised and Updated

DAWN DAIS

SEAL PRESS

New York

Seal Press
Hachette Book Group
1290 Avenue of the Americas, New York, NY 10104
www.sealpress.com
@sealpress

Printed in the United States of America

First Trade Paperback Edition: June 2013

Second Trade Paperback Edition: November 2021

Published by Seal Press, an imprint of Perseus Books, LLC, a subsidiary of Hachette Book Group, Inc. The Seal Press name and logo is a trademark of the Hachette Book Group.

The Hachette Speakers Bureau provides a wide range of authors for speaking events. To find out more, go to www.hachettespeakersbureau.com or call (866) 376-6591.

The publisher is not responsible for websites (or their content) that are not owned by the publisher.

Print book interior design by Amy Quinn.

Library of Congress Cataloging-in-Publication Data
Names: Dais, Dawn, author.
Title: The sh!t no one tells you : a guide to surviving your baby's first year / Dawn Dais.
Other titles: Shit no one tells you
Description: Second trade paperback edition. | New York : Seal Press, 2021.
Identifiers: LCCN 2021020370 | ISBN 9781541620353 (paperback) | ISBN 9781541620773 (ebook)
Subjects: LCSH: Motherhood—Humor. | Infants—Humor. | Child rearing—Humor.
Classification: LCC HQ759 .D245 2021 | DDC 306.874/3—dc23
LC record available at https://lccn.loc.gov/2021020370

ISBNs: 9781541620353 (paperback), 9781541620773 (ebook)

LSC-C

Printing 1, 2021

To Vivian, who kicked my ass and stole my heart

CONTENTS

Contents

HELLO FROM THE OTHER SIDE

(an Introduction to my Introduction)

Many years ago, I decided I wanted to write a book about the first months with my first baby. I had spent the better part of my baby's newborn phase repeatedly lamenting/rage-whispering, "Why didn't anyone tell me about all this shit?!" I wanted to write a book because knew I wasn't the only new parent rage-whispering themselves into a frenzy. I also knew I could fill roughly 842 pages with the amount of shit no one told me about babies before I was allowed to leave the hospital with one.

I finally got around to writing the book when my first child was eighteen months old and I was four months pregnant with baby number two. My eighteen-month-old still wasn't a great sleeper, I was juggling (mostly fumbling) work and parenthood, and I was blessed with all-day morning sickness the entire time I was writing this book. This is all to say, I was still very much IN IT when *The Sh!t No One Tells You* came to fruition. Honestly, the entire book-writing experience feels a bit like a fever dream that somehow ended up in bookstores.

In the time between then and now, *The Sh!t No One Tells You* has found a sizable audience of new parents who are also very much IN IT. The pages of this book reflect a messy, confusing, overwhelming time in my life, and I think that mess is relatable for the new parents who read it. (The profanity on the cover is probably pretty relatable as well.)

My kids are now ten and eight years old, and when I read this book today, it feels rough around the edges and raw in a way that can appear a bit harsh. My description of breastfeeding makes it sound like I was dropped into a combat zone; the obsession with baby bodily functions is more than a little concerning. I speak of sleep as if it is an ex who left me unexpectedly, an ex I'm clearly not over. I'm tempted to do a thorough edit of the text, to bring it more in line with the way I feel now that I'm well beyond the overwhelming baby years.

But that's not what this book is supposed to be. It's not supposed to be a watered-down version of new parenthood, told to you by someone who is in a completely different parenting season. If you are reading this book, the odds are you are very much in the hurricane season of parenthood. You want to read about the mess, because you are in the mess, too.

So instead of altering my messy take on parenthood I decided to add a few features based on the feedback I've heard over the years. A lot of partners have reached out after reading this book and appreciated its candor, so I've littered Partner Corners throughout the chapters to provide insight and advice for the dads who are drawn in by the word "Sh!t" on the cover. I've also added a chapter for single mommas because they kick a tremendous amount of ass and need to be recognized. I brought the rest of the book up to the present, included more tips I wish I had known, and generally tried to up the information provided without diminishing the complete and utter chaos depicted.

But before we get started on the chaos, I want to share with you a little bit of sage advice. I've learned a lot over my years of parenting, but I really have only two things I wish I had known from the beginning.

1. Take videos: This advice isn't really going to make or break your parenting success rate. But it is something that will provide you such joy when you are no longer IN IT and have moved into the season of parenting when you are accosting new parents with promises that *it all goes by so fast*.

    Without fail you will take roughly 38,563 pictures of your baby in his or her first year. When you come across those pictures down the road you will, without fail, ooo and aww over each one. But I'm here to tell you that videos are so much better than photos when it comes to ooo-ing and aww-ing.

There's something about videos that perfectly captures the specificity of childhood moments. The indelible sound of their little voices and coos, the way they kick their chubby legs or contour their facial expressions, your exhausted voice in the background chatting with the baby as though you are actually participating in a two-way conversation.

Take the videos and get in the videos with them, too. Keep the videos on your phone or post them to only yourself on your social media. I promise you many an ooo and aww will await you in a few years when you come across them and realize how *worth it* this crazy time was.

2. Lower your expectations: Here's the thing. You've been given the job of creating an entire human being from scratch. I get it. It's a *really* big deal. You want to do your best and be the best for this little human. You have very high expectations, and you are the kind of person who regularly meets high expectations. But you are going to need to bring those expectations down a little bit. And then down a bit more.

Parenting is a really hard gig, and it's made even more difficult by the expectations we put on ourselves. It is not easy for anyone, not even for the social media moms who make it look easy with their carefully curated greatest hits posts. Just remember, if it's hard and messy and overwhelming, if it's the complete opposite of photo worthy, you are doing it right. You will have good days and bad days and days that make you question every life choice you've ever made. But on all those days, please give yourself grace. And give that little human grace as well. Your child may hit some milestones later than other kids. You may regularly drop several of the four hundred balls you are trying to juggle. Bathing may become an alarmingly rare occurrence. All that is okay. You are okay. Everything is okay. Because all expectations have been lowered, and then lowered still.

As you venture into the rest of this book, and into my description of navigating the first year with my first baby, I'll leave you with this: I promise you it gets better. No phase lasts forever. And when all else fails, never underestimate the benefit of a well-executed rage whisper.

Now, on to the mess.

INTRODUCTION

At some point during the first few weeks with their new bundle of joy, every parent will most likely utter/scream/sigh/ cry out into the night, "I had no idea it was going to be this hard!" This is because a vast conspiracy exists to hide the truth from all who have yet to bring home a baby, for fear that if the truth were to get out, people would (1) stop having babies or (2) stop bringing them home. I am here to end that silence. And replace it with a lot of bitching.

Before I had a baby I would see those Johnson & Johnson commercials where a mom is gleefully giving her perfect and beautiful smiling baby a bath in the sink. Splashing and giggles ensue. The tagline for the commercial is "Having a baby changes everything." I used to well up with emotion when I watched that commercial, knowing that when I had a baby she would change everything, too. And by "changes everything," I thought they meant "changes the things you clean in the sink." Turns out by "everything," they actually mean everything. As in, "your entire life—we are not joking."

Now that I have a child, I believe their point would have been better conveyed if the baby were screaming at the top of his lungs in the sink while a mom with alarmingly dark circles under her eyes stared off into the distance blankly, unaware that the water from the sink was being emptied onto the floor by her splash-happy child. I well up with emotion just thinking of that scenario.

Don't get me wrong—I love my child more deeply than I ever thought I had the capacity to, but it's not all giggles and playful splashing. I actually think the most difficult part of new parenting is the conflicting emotions you feel and your fear of even acknowledging those different emotions, let alone sharing them. I planned and prayed for my baby for years before she arrived. When I found out I was pregnant, I was ecstatic. Holding her for the first time was unreal. But then we got her home, and the day-to-day realities of caring for a newborn started to sink in. This is when I started thinking, *I had no idea it was going to be this hard.*

I felt guilty that I wasn't loving every second and that I didn't look or feel anything like I thought an ecstatic new mother should. Of course, I had expected it to be hard, but somehow not *this* hard. I blame my lack of information on my friends who had children before me. When I told them I was pregnant, all I heard was "Congrats!" and "Yippee!!" Never did any of them say, "Hold on to your f'n hat. Shit's about to get real." Sure, it would have been the first time any of them had ever said, "Shit's about to get real," but I feel like it would have been the perfect time to christen the phrase.

Instead, I went blindly into parenthood, with no idea of what was coming my way. It was months before I really talked to anyone about how overwhelmed I was. Up until that point I was a little ashamed at the idea of complaining about having the healthy baby I had dreamed of for so many years. But when I finally started talking to other moms, they all agreed without hesitation that having a new baby is ridiculously hard. They then instantly bombarded me with tales of their own struggles. This gave me comfort, but mostly it pissed me off. "How come you didn't warn me about any of this??!!!"

So that is what I've set out to do with this book. Warn you about all the shit no one is telling you. My intention is not to frighten you or to scare you off having children. My hope is to give you what I didn't have: the ability to say, "I am not the only parent in the history of the planet to have their ass handed to them by something they could fit in a purse." Knowing you are not alone actually helps a little. Trust me, misery does love company, especially during 3:00 a.m. feeding sessions.

To add to your company, I've enlisted the help of a few of my mom friends to share their stories as well. My "Moms on the Front Lines" are reporting live from the battlefields of parenting. They've built up heavy armor over the years and gotten quick at side-stepping land mines. They have come here to share their inspiring tales of survival. (None have teenagers yet, however, so I can make no long-term guarantees for their well-being.)

The early days of new parenthood have a way of covering your life in a thick fog. It's confounding and overwhelming, and it can be difficult to see anything besides what is right in front of you. *The Sh!t No One Tells You*, with its honest advice and dispatches from the front, is your reminder that the fog is not permanent, and even though it can feel like it, you are not alone in your utter disorientation. As you navigate the challenging first year with a new baby, we will be here to encourage you (and bitch with you, of course).

Go ahead. Stumble through the first year of sleepless nights and poop-filled days, and carry this book with you often (keeping it a safe distance away from the poop, if at all possible). I've purposely made very little effort to organize the chapters of this book. Jump around from chapter to chapter, depending on what you happen to be dealing with on any given day. And with your impending memory loss (see Chapter 26, "Remember Your Memory?," for more info on this subject), you'll be able to read the book seven or eight times before actually realizing you're finished! So many good times ahead for you.

So, let's head out on this parenting adventure together, shall we? There will be ups, downs, tears, and vomit. And that's just the childbirth. Because, as I warned you before, shit's about to get real . . .

MY MOMS ON THE FRONT LINES

There is no one right way to do anything when it comes to parenting, which is one of the most frustrating things about it. What works for your best friend and her child might not work for you (and honestly, probably only works about 75 percent of the time for your best friend). Although I'm the one writing a book about parenting, I know there are a lot of other opinions and stories out there.

That's where my Moms on the Front Lines come in, referred to collectively throughout the book as my MOFLs. I've known all these women for years and asked them to contribute a little insight into different parenting styles, struggles, and stories. They gave me so much more than I could have ever hoped for.

While all our families and situations are a little different, the MOFLs have a lot in common. We all love our kids to pieces, we have a sense of humor about life in general, and none of us have any

11

idea how and when we became grown-ups who have been left responsible for small children. It's troubling, to say the least.

Before we get started, I wanted to introduce you to my moms, with some of their stats (age, age of kids, years married, plans for more kids), so you know who the players are.

Me, Dawn: Age thirty-five. "I have one daughter, age eighteen months, and another child is due soon. I've been with my partner, Becky, for five years. I work from home part time most of the time (except when I'm on deadline for a parenting book) and will probably continue to do so until my kids are in school (or until I start writing my next book about dealing with a newborn and the terrible twos at the same time)."

Chipper Jen:* Age thirty-five. "I have a son who is four and a daughter who is two. I've been married five years to a guy I've known since high school. I'm a stay-at-home mom who is never home (I keep the kids very busy). I work two nights a week bartending so I can have an adult conversation, but I actually end up taking care of drunks whose behavior is worse than my children's. My husband works a lot and is always *amazed* at how the birthday

---

* For those of you who read my first book, *The Nonrunner's Marathon Guide for Women*, you'll remember my friend Chipper Jen. I call her Chipper Jen because she is chipper as hell about everything in life, whether it be running 26.2 miles or birthin' babies. She had two children by the time my first came along, so she became my go-to for frantic "I don't know what the hell I'm doing" text messages all hours of the day and night during my baby's first year. She was always quick with a response and calming words. I hope you all have a Chipper Jen in your life, but if you don't, she has plenty to share in the coming pages.

parties, holidays, and family functions just 'happen'! No, I'm not having any more kids!"

Amy L.: Age thirty-five. "I have two daughters, a four-year-old and a one-year-old. I've been married for ten years. I'm a teacher, and I work full-time, although juggling both is hard. I love being a mom, but at my first appointment with my second pregnancy I made sure to ask about options for future sterilization. (My husband took the plunge and got snipped nine days after the baby was born. PHEW.)"

Amy W.: Age thirty-six. "I almost have three kids (all boys): seven, three, and one due next year. My husband and I have been married for nine years, and we were married for only one before we got pregnant with the first baby. I'm a stay-at-home mom, but I do work part time (eight to twelve hours a week) when my husband can be with the kids. Not sure if this baby will be the last one. I'll let you know in two years."

Carrie: Age thirty-three. "I've been married for five years. I have two kids, ages two and a half and five months, both boys. We waited three years before kids, and I stayed home for one year with the first, then worked full-time for a year. Now I am home again. I continue to do contract work and serve on a nonprofit board. I'm not sure what the future holds, work-wise, but no more babies. Our family is complete."

Dana: Age thirty-three. "I have two kids (a two-and-a-half-year-old girl and four-month-old boy). I've been married for seven years.

I work full time and I'm not sure yet if we are done having kids. We'll see!"

Erika: Age thirty-four. "I have one kid, age twenty-one months, and one on the way. I've been married three and a half years. We started trying right away. We got pregnant immediately but miscarried the first time. I work full time but from home mostly (though the kid is still in daycare all day). I went back to work the first time after four and a half months, but only part time at first, and had the baby in daycare only part time as well. I plan to do the same with the second kid if possible (financially). We have no plans for more kids after these two."

Jenine: Age thirty-five. "I have two kids, a four-year-old girl and a one-and-a-half-year-old boy. I've been married six years, together eleven! My husband has made sure that we are done with kids (with my permission, he did it as soon as I said it was okay). I've been home for four years and will be for another one or two until the little one is in preschool."

Jill: Age forty-one. "I have two kids (Noah and T.J., twins, six and a half years old). I've been married for thirteen years, and I just returned to work after taking a six-year break to be at home with my kids. No more kids are planned although I'd love more."

Karen: Age thirty-nine. "I'm a single mom with full custody. My daughter, Mikayla, is three. I work sixty hours or so a week and travel probably one week every two months. Probably no more kids because of medical reasons."

Melanie: Age thirty-seven. "I have one son who is nearly three. I was married four and a half years before our unplanned and loving boy arrived. I went back to work full time after six weeks, then took another six weeks off when my son was six months old. I'm undecided about more children, for many reasons, but finances and house size are two factors."

Michelle: Age thirty-one. "I have one boy who's almost two, and another boy who's due next year. I've been married for six years, together for twelve. I'm currently working four days a week but would love to be a stay-at-home mom."

Monica: Age thirty-five. "I have four kids. Sam is seven, Cali is six (those two are nineteen months apart). Four years later came Hailey, who is two; eighteen and a half months later came Jackson, who is seven months old. Sam was nine months old when B.J. and I got married. I got pregnant one month later with my second. Neither of my first children were planned, but in the end it's been 'the plan' all along."

Salpy: Age thirty-seven. "I have four kids: ages eight, six, two and a half, and three months. I've been married for thirteen years. I worked as a teacher before having kids, then decided to stay home with them. Not planning on having any more kids."

Sarah B.: Age thirty-four. "I have two boys (Andrew is three years old, and Owen is three months old). My other 'kids' are Audrey (fourteen, cat), Rudy (thirteen, cat), and Jack (six, dog). We will not be having any more! I've been married for six years, and we were together fifteen years before kids. I am returning to work when Owen is four and a half months. The first month I will be part time and then full time after that."

Sarah G.: Age thirty-three. "I have two boys, ages nine and six and a half, and a little girl who is two and a half. I've been married twelve and a half years. I was a stay-at-home mom for the first four and a half years, until the economy took a dump. Now I work full time. We are not planning on having any more kids. We also have one dog, one cat, and four fish tanks. Super moms CAN do it all (with the help of housekeepers, gardeners, full-time nannies, and carpools). It literally takes a village to raise my family!!!" Another note I received from Sarah: "Some entertaining postscript for your book. Man gets vasectomy on Monday. Woman takes positive pregnancy test on Saturday. Yup, I'm pregnant with our fourth child. Still in shock."

Sommer: Age thirty-four. "I have one baby who is fifteen months old. I've been married two years, six months before we had the baby. I'm a stay-at-home everything."

There are a few other moms who pop up throughout the book, women who gave me their take on various subjects along the way, but the moms above are those whose names you are going to see the most on the following pages. I hope all our stories can help guide you a bit through your first year of motherhood.

THE PARTNERS

Most baby books speak directly to new moms, since it's believed that new moms make up a majority of the baby book audience. That may be true, but based on the number of partners who have reached out to me over the years, it is not just the moms who are skimming baby books, frantically looking for directions on their new uncharted road.

I decided to bring some partner voices into *The Sh!t No One Tells You* to advise on some of the major parenting tasks. I was pleasantly surprised by the responses I received from the guys I reached out to. They were honest and open, vulnerable and funny. A lot of times partners can take a little longer to find their footing with a new baby, but that should never be confused with lack of investment in the project at hand. The partners featured in this book are great examples of guys who take their role and responsibility very seriously.

I hope the Partner Corners in this book can provide some camaraderie for the partners, as well as a bit of insight for the moms who are reading. Early days of parenting can be like heading off to

THE SH!T NO ONE TELLS YOU

battle. The baby is the bomb, but a lot of times couples can turn on each other in the foxhole. You are both tired and rattled, and yelling at the child is not an option. So before you turn your sleep-deprivation rage on each other, take a deep breath, read some Partner Corners, and agree that the only shot you two grown adults have is to work together to operate the very tiny human.

Here are the dads you will see sharing their thoughts throughout the book. I asked them each to share something that scared them before their first baby arrived:

Jason: Jason has been married ten years and has a six-year-old son. "I was scared to death of having a kid! I'd never changed a diaper. I didn't know what to do with a little human. The doctor and midwife stayed with us for a few hours after his birth. When they wanted to leave, both my wife and I panicked. We had no idea what to do with a little kid and realized we should've read the manual BEFORE he was born! We begged for help and called my sister, who has two kids, over."

Larry: Larry has been married ten years. He and his wife have two kids, a girl, age eight, and a boy, age four. "I was scared about finishing my last year of school and being a supportive husband and father. Of the three, school took a back seat. In reality I should have just taken the year off of school to dedicate all my efforts to the sleepless child rearing."

Pat: Pat has been married three years. His daughter is two years old. "I was scared of being a father!!! Truly, it terrified me. I was scared of how it would change the dynamics of our marriage.

Would we ever sleep again? How would it impact us financially? All of those thoughts were terrifying."

Tom: Tom has been married sixteen years and has two girls (ages ten and twelve). "Hmm, not so much scared as concerned. We were concerned that for as much planning and reading we did, we still had no clue what to do. I even have video of my wife holding our first daughter hours after her birth. As the camera zooms in on our daughter's face, you can hear my wife off camera ask, 'What do we DO with her??' (Full disclosure, we STILL don't have the answer.)"

THE SH!T
NO ONE TELLS YOU

1

AND YOU THOUGHT PREGNANCY WAS HARD

(you were such a wimp)

Pre-Baby:

"I can't sleep because there is a baby on my bladder."

Post-Baby:

"I can't sleep because there is a baby on my boob."

Pre-Baby:

"All my clothes consist of 95 percent elastic."

Post-Baby:

"All my clothes consist of 95 percent spit-up."

Pre-Baby:

"I look adorably nine months pregnant."

Post-Baby:

"I look not so adorably five months pregnant (for a year)."

For the first twenty weeks of my pregnancy, I felt like I was going to puke twenty-four hours a day. I had to force food down and take deep, concentrated breaths between each bite to make sure it stayed down. After that five-month adventure, things got easier, although I was absolutely exhausted all the time, as if my body had all the energy wrung out of it. Then, in my third trimester the baby started her regular gymnastics practices on my bladder and ribs concurrently. Toward the very end, sitting was quite uncomfortable, as was sleeping, standing, and keeping a full bladder for more than three minutes at a time.

Like many pregnant women, I was very ready for my baby to make her appearance outside of my body after slowly taking over the inside for forty weeks. Then, a few weeks after she came kicking into the world, I thought to myself, *Holy shitballs, pregnancy was so easy compared to this!*

So here's the thing. If you haven't yet popped your baby out, you need to maximize every second of pre-poppage that you can. Trust me, you'll thank me later.

First, go take an uncomfortable nap. In a little while you will be longing for sleep of any kind, uncomfortable or otherwise. After your nap, go out to dinner. Order an appetizer and a dessert. Tell the waiter to take their time, no rush. Then go to a movie. Sure, you will probably sleep through most of it and have heartburn the rest of the time, but be strong! While you are out and about you will notice people being extra kind and attentive toward you because you are pregnant. You've probably noticed that for a while. Milk it. In a very short time you will go back to being treated like everyone else, which is ironic, because that's when you'll actually need the most help.

When you get home, don't go to bed. Instead, curl up on your couch and flip through the channels. Watch whatever you want, for as long as you want. Do yourself a favor and pick something with cuss words. Again, you will probably fall asleep, but that is fine. The general rule is always: If you want to fall asleep the last few weeks of pregnancy, fall asleep. Wherever, whenever—just sleep.

Eventually drag your fat butt to bed and curl up for a slumber that will be interrupted only by general discomfort and the need to pee. Sleep in as late as you want, and then sleep later than that. Hell, don't even get out of bed all day. Order delivery, watch crappy TV, read a book, spend hours on the phone talking about absolutely nothing with friends and family.

All the while be sure to realize that no matter how bloated and stiff and sore and exhausted you may feel now, this is the best you are going to feel in a very, very long time.

Cheers!

2

PLEASE CENSOR YOUR BIRTH STORY

(please)

How to tell your birth story

- To a group of mothers: "Here is every single detail."

- To an expectant mother: "Yep, just fell right out."

- To a teenage girl: "It was so much worse than I was expecting."

- To your child (in fifteen years): "Here is every single detail, with extra emphasis on the pain part."

- To a man: "The stork brought me a baby."

Here's the thing. Childbirth is gnarly. There is a reason that TV shows portray the childbirth process as basically (1) minor contractions, (2) three sweaty pushes, (3) happy, clean baby all wrapped up in his mother's arms. A true representation of childbirth would not be suitable for broadcast under FCC regulations. The general public isn't built to withstand the details of childbirth. So please proceed accordingly when sharing your own tales of birthing.

When you are telling your birth story, please, for the love of all things holy and pure, take your audience into consideration before going too deep with the details. Unless you are sitting in a room full of new mothers and midwives, perhaps leave out the part about the placenta. In fact, anything involving blood and/or tearing can be completely skipped most of the time, for most audiences.

Say it with me now: "I, [your name here], will not post any birth story details on social media that may cause eye and/or brain damage to my poor unsuspecting cyberfriends, many of whom haven't seen me in years and don't really need to know any details AT ALL about my whooha."

I will give you an example of how to proceed correctly. First, I will start with my birth story.

I woke up around 3:00 a.m. with what I thought were perhaps contractions. My due date wasn't for another week, so I wasn't sure it was really happening. Not wanting to get too excited or wake my partner from a peaceful slumber for what could have turned out to be gas, I counted the minutes between each contraction and after about an hour concluded that things were really happening.

I rolled over and woke up my partner. "I think it's Baby Day."

She instantly popped out of bed and started packing our (already packed) hospital bag. Somehow the only way to control her nervousness was by overpreparing for our hospital stay. The dogs were quite annoyed at the early-morning distraction.

I just lay in the bed and contracted periodically. We grabbed a pen and paper and started marking down how far apart the contractions were and how long they were lasting. This was a great job for Becky because it gave her something to do after nothing else would fit in the bag.

We had been told we needed to wait until "5-1-1" before going to the hospital: contractions five minutes apart, lasting one minute, for one hour. More than anything we did NOT want to be the people who got to the hospital early and were sent home because the baby was nowhere near ready. The hospital was a good half-hour drive away, and we only wanted to make that trek once.

The contractions continued pretty steadily for a few hours. At about 6:00 a.m., I called my parents to let them know we were moving forward. "It's Baby Day!" They were very excited, but my mother also cautioned, "This could be false labor, so don't get too worked up just yet." Thanks, Mom.

I texted my friends to let them know what was going on. Chipper Jen also warned that it could be false labor.

Around 7:00 a.m., my contractions leveled off. They were no longer consistent, and I was no longer amused. I was sitting on the damn birthing ball in the living room, ready for to get this show on the road, and the show had all but stopped. Since I had been up for too many hours already, I decided I was done with this nonsense went back to bed.

Becky was excited that she had more time to finish some last-minute projects she had planned for the week before the due date. She called her brother over to the house, and they began doing random home improvement in the baby's room. Which seems like a fantastic way to deal with a possible childbirth happening in the next room.

When I woke up from my nap around 10:00 a.m., I didn't even bother to time the contractions I was having. I was still pissed at the false alarm from earlier and was convinced that this was more of the same. Jen and my mom tried to comfort me via phone and text messaging, letting me know my body would get there when it was ready. They believed I was having contractions, but they also believed (and so did I) that my extremely low tolerance for pain was working me up and making me a bit dramatic.

Then things got a little more serious. I got up and went to the bathroom and found what I had to assume was the mucus plug, because it definitely lived up to its very descriptive name. I got back into bed and texted Jen, who told me you can lose your mucus plug days or weeks before you actually deliver. So I tried to go back to sleep.

The contractions were getting much more painful at this point, and I was trying to time them by myself as I was going through them. Becky was next door in her office (our offices are in the actual house next door) trying to get some work done. I texted her about my progress. She said would wrap up work and head back over.

A little while later I got up again to go to the bathroom and my water broke. Because I had tested positive for strep B, I knew it was officially time to get to the hospital. I texted Becky again. When she finally came back, she was delightfully unaware of the status of my labor. "Can I take a shower real quick?" I shrugged through a contraction and said okay.

I went into the dining room and sat down at the table with my head in my hands. The pain was getting pretty bad. Our neighbor, Michelle, came over to check on me. In the course of our minute-long conversation, I had two contractions. "Wait, are your contractions that close?"

I nodded yes. "But they aren't lasting a whole minute. It's 5-1-1, so they have to be lasting a minute before it's serious." Michelle ran into the bedroom and screamed at Becky to get the hell out of the shower.

Becky and Michelle helped me walk to the car in what was the longest walk of my life. The walk was followed by the longest car ride of my life. We took Becky's Range Rover, a car that likes to think of itself as sporty. And apparently "sporty" cars don't need "real" shocks. I could feel every damn pebble we ran over on that twenty-five-minute high-speed chase down the freeway. I wear hearing aids, and without them I can't hear much. I took them out of my ears, because sound was just too much at the time. I arched my back and tried so hard to get away from what was happening. I started saying "Fuuuuuuuuck" over and over again. (Becky will tell you I started *screaming* "Fuuuuuuuuck." I can neither confirm nor deny this claim.)

The only thing that gave me any solace during this ride was the image of my friend Jodi, whose labor I had been at. She was having terrible contractions in the hospital, and then the Epidural Man came around and she took a three-hour nap. I just kept telling myself, "When I get to the hospital I get a nap. When I get to the hospital I get a nap."

We got to the hospital, parked in the drop-off area, and Becky grabbed a nearby wheelchair to wheel me in. I am planning to file some sort of class-action lawsuit against the designers of these wheelchairs, if you would like to get in on my case. This metal wheelchair was like a medieval torture device that I was forced into while a child was pushing her way out of my body. As I sat down, I spotted those yellow bumps on the ground before the door and screamed, "No, wait, wait until this contraction—"

Becky did not wait and pushed me in that metal torture device over the horrendous bumps. Wow, that was fun. She then wheeled me into the delivery center and we were instantly motioned past check-in to the secured baby-birthing area. I have been told I might have been screaming.

When we got to the nurses, they slowed everything down. "Hello there, here is some paperwork to fill out."

Becky tried to move it along. "This is her first child. She's in a lot of pain."

Apparently the nurses at the hospital also thought I merely had a low tolerance for pain, because they didn't seem all that concerned about my situation. One nurse handed Becky a clipboard of paperwork to fill out while another one rolled me into the bathroom. Once we were in there, she handed me a pee cup and said, "I need you to stand over the toilet and catch your urine midstream in this cup."

I looked at her as if she had asked me to do a backflip and then pee in a cup. "Um, I can't stand up. And I definitely can't pee in that cup."

The nurse was unimpressed. She wheeled me into a room where I undressed, and they got me into a bed. There was clicking on computers, calmness all around. I looked to Becky, who was sweating profusely. I begged her to do something.

"Will there be a doctor here soon?" Becky asked.

"The doctor is on her way down, don't worry."

I was worried. I knew I needed a doctor to authorize my drugs, and I knew more than anything I needed my drugs. Becky stepped away for a second and checked her blood. She is diabetic and was feeling a bit light headed. As she was checking, she pleaded with the nurse, "Can someone please check her dilation?"

In what I believe was an attempt to shut us up, the nurse agreed to check my dilation. And that's when things went nutballs.

"Okay, well, you are at nine centimeters, so . . ." she said way too calmly, considering there was only one centimeter to go before this thing was over.

I looked to Becky, hoping against hope that with my poor hearing I had just heard that wrong. "What did she just say?"

"Nine."

I instantly started to cry. I knew what this meant. "Can I still get drugs???"

"We'll see," the nurse lied, dashing all hopes of a nap.

I looked at Becky, who was trying to comfort me while shoving Skittles in her mouth. I asked her what her blood sugar was. She said nonchalantly, "It was thirty; it's fine."

This was another unfortunate number, seeing as her blood sugar should be between 80 and 180, and 50 is considered very low. This number was so alarming that my nine centimeters of childbirthing took a backseat for a second. The scrambling nurses started scrambling to find food for Becky, while others were scrambling to find a doctor for me.

I got wheeled toward the delivery room just as the food arrived and Becky started shoving it into her face. She was left to pick up all the food, my clothes, our hospital bag, and her purse and rush after me, all while trying to avoid diabetic shock. As I was being pushed into the delivery room, as if on cue, I could feel the baby start pushing out of me, and I was overwhelmed with the urge to help her along. There were so many drugs involved in how I imagined this moment was going to go, and so few drugs happening right now. I freaked out even more.

The nurse told Becky she should call anyone who was supposed to be there for the birth, because the baby was coming very soon. Becky called my parents, who raced over to the hospital.

Meanwhile, I was losing my mind in the delivery room, still asking if there was any way to get some drugs involved. No one would tell me no, because they thought it would make me even more crazy, but I don't think that was possible. One nurse said, "If we give you drugs now, it will hurt the baby." I wondered how *much* it would hurt the baby . . .

Roughly thirteen thousand people entered the room and started turning on machines and trying to hook me up to them. My main nurse, Ann, was trying desperately to attach some sort of something to my belly. It was a monitor of some sort, and she felt the need to push it hard against my stomach *right* when I was having a contraction in that very location. I kept hitting her hands away and asking why she insisted on doing that when I was contracting. I'm pretty sure her goal was to actually monitor the baby during my contractions, but I was too busy trying to talk her into waiting until after I was in pain. This did not make Ann's job easy.

My mom joined the party as it was getting into full swing. There were nurses and doctors everywhere, I was flailing everywhere, and Becky had no idea what the hell to do. I had gone completely off the rails because my brain could not process the thought of doing all this without drugs. The nurses and doctors were nervous because they couldn't get a reading on the baby and had no idea what was going on with her. At the time, I didn't know why they were nervous, but it was making me nervous as well. Which made me even crazier.

At one point, fed up with my lunacy, Ann grabbed my face and told me once and for all, "No, you are not getting drugs. Now stop listening to anyone but me and do what I tell you." Ann was a little bit of a hard-ass, but I needed that.

Next she told me not to push, but the baby was moving and I couldn't stop it. "I'm pushing." "Don't push." "I'm pushing."

When they told me to grab my legs to push, I arched my back with my arms up above my head, still trying to somehow get away from the pain. Finally, Becky and my mom got on either side of me and pushed me forward to try to get me to where I was supposed to be. Then I started pushing.

I don't remember this part being any more traumatic than the rest, other than when "You're going to feel a little—" *Sliiiice.* There was nothing "little" about what I felt.

I was holding my mom's hand at the time and took her thumb so far back I had to stop myself because even in my crazed state I knew it was about to break. (Side note to anyone going in to support a woman during childbirth: I don't recommend giving her ONLY your thumb to hold on to; it could end very poorly.) I screamed at the top of my lungs, "Why would you do that??!!" The woman had just sliced my whooha for God's sake. That was uncalled for.

Apparently they really wanted the baby out because they weren't able to monitor her, and after three pushes, she wasn't budging. So a slice was in order.

One more push and her head came out, another push and the rest of her popped out. She came out kicking, like she had been doing for months on my bladder and ribs. The four hundred people in the room swept her to the side to check her out and make sure everything was fine, while I lay back in the bed and just shook my head.

We had been there for less than an hour. Oh my goodness, what just happened?

A little while later a nurse came over to check me in, since they hadn't had enough time to do so before the craziness started. She asked me all the questions you ask a woman who is in labor, but hasn't yet had the baby. Including "Do you have a birth plan?"

I looked at her and laughed. "Yes, and it just had the word 'drugs' written all over it, so I don't think the birth went quite as planned."

So that is my birth story, the long version. The version that I've told close family and very close friends.

Here is the version I put on Facebook:

On the way to the hospital, to save myself from having to text everyone *and* scream f-bombs at the same time: "Heading to the hospital! Pray for us. And for lots of drugs."

After the baby popped out: "People. Your prayers were not focused. Baby is perfect. But I got here too late for drugs!!! Nine centimeters when I checked in!!! Holy crap. It was quick, though. Welcome to the world, Baby Vivian!"

Looking back, I think maybe even mentioning nine centimeters was a little too much information to put on the interweb. Hopefully anyone who didn't know what I was referring to didn't take it upon themselves to investigate further.

Here is the version I tell people I don't know very well: "I was wheeled into the hospital screaming my face off and an hour later my baby was born. It was insane." The end. No talk of pushing or slicing or screaming or what comes out after the baby does, just a good old-fashioned G-rated birthin' story.

Also, steer clear of enlightening pregnant women with your birthing details. You may think you are doing them a favor by answering their questions honestly, but really, unless you can say, "I was walking along, and oops, out popped a baby!" they probably don't actually want to know the truth.

Before I gave birth, I had several friends tell me about their labor experiences. I gobbled up the info like I was studying for a pop quiz. ("Pop" being the key word there.) But the thing is, there is no way to prepare someone for their individual birth experience, because each one is like its own profanity-laced snowflake. Despite all my studying, I didn't get my drugs when I went pop. Some women want natural childbirth but have to get an emergency C-section. And others think they will be Zen warriors with Enya playing, but end up strangling their husbands in a birthing tub. Shit can go sideways, is my point.

If you haven't had your baby yet, here is the only thing I can tell you to calm your fears. Before I had my baby I would repeatedly—repeatedly—tell people that my biggest fear (beyond something bad happening to the baby, of course) was that I would get to the hospital too late to get drugs. I said it repeatedly. And guess what? My biggest fear came true. And guess what? I survived. I felt every second of that child kicking her way out of me and I didn't puke or pass out from the pain (I might have headed those things off with my frequent f-bombs). And at the end I had a perfect little baby . . . and stitches in my whooha.

No matter what your birth entails, you will get through it. It's going to be painful and ugly and somewhat humiliating. And yet, it will become one of the most beautiful moments of your life. Who knew beauty could be so messy?

In the spirit of messiness, I asked my MOFLs to tell me something fun about their labor.

Michelle says, "I went from three-quarter centimeters to ten in less than two hours. No time for an epidural!"

Chipper Jen's husband apparently is not as energetic as she is. "My husband was snoring on the little pullout couch while I was about to barf from anxiety because I was about to give birth to a watermelon!"

Sarah heard this during her delivery: "Ma'am, it looks like you are ready to push, but we are really understaffed, so can you wait one hour?"

Monica had an interesting first delivery. "My family calls me cave woman because I wanted to be completely naked for my first labor. I was trying everything to get Sam out. The pull-up bar thing, Indian squats—you name it, I tried it. I pushed for one hour and twenty minutes."

Carrie says, "I labored and delivered in the tub with my second. I remember seeing a little fish net and thinking, *I'm delivering a kid, not a fish here, people.* Then halfway through pushing, I realized what the little net was for: poop. Looking back it kind of grosses me out."

On a side note, while I continue to beg you to censor your own battle stories, I also advise you that this is what will happen if you ever ask a group of moms to share theirs. Lots of details with a lot of unfortunate visuals will happen. Be forewarned.

PARTNER CORNER: CHILDBIRTH

Pat: My wife bought me books and kept sending me articles about birth and what to expect. But the only thing that helped me was going to a natural birthing class. My wife wanted as natural a birth as possible, without pain meds, so going to this style of class helped me understand the different phases of the birthing process, how long labor can be, and what I could do as a partner for my wife. A lot of people don't understand that it's really you and your partner in the room for a majority of the time. Nurses come and go, and you only see the doctor for maybe the final twenty minutes. So, bring your laptop, snacks, music, and aromatherapy because it could be two days or longer before you see your baby.

Larry: Do: Ask questions so she can guide you. Don't: Ask too many questions or express your opinion unless it's asked for.

Tom: Videotape it landscape style, not portrait—don't be an amateur. Honestly, other than comforting the mom-to-be, do what YOU are comfortable with. If you want to witness the birth (and your wife is fine with it), then do it; if you feel that just being there is joy enough that you don't need to see crowning and all that comes next (and want to save some modicum of mystery in your marriage), feel free to stand by your wife's shoulder and hold her hand. Don't be guilted into thinking one way is better than the other.

3

RAID THE HOSPITAL

(get the most out of that health plan)

Total cost of all the stuff you take home from the hospital: $8,547,253

Not having to make some poor loved one stand in a checkout line holding nether-region numbing spray, mesh underpants, and pillow-size maxi pads:
Priceless

I have found that women have varying experiences during their hospital stays post-childbirth, ranging from peaceful to pending lawsuit. I'm here to tell you that no matter what your experience, you need to stay focused on what is important. And that is raiding the hospital for everything that isn't nailed down.

Yes, you have $350 million worth of baby whatnots waiting for you at home, but that is no reason to pass up another $5 million in free loot that the hospital provides. You are scavenging for the good of your child! It's primal, really.

When we were in the hospital, we were almost pathological about how much stuff we tried to fit into our "labor bag." Our addiction started simply enough, like so many do: just a little blanket here, an oversize maxi pad there. Then it got out of control. We stayed a couple of extra nights at the hospital because Vivian was a little underweight, and during those nights we got into a bit of a baby-care routine. That routine required the use of many hospital items, so to make sure we could replicate the routine at home, we deduced that we had to bring the hospital home with us. Obviously. Our stripping the room of all valuables was gradual, starting with a few little things every day that would be replaced by the nurses, allowing us to make another pass-through later. The last thing I saw being shoved into our bag was the industrial-size hand sanitizer squirter. Because obviously a hospital would have the *best* hand sanitizer around—to ward off all the germs that infest that place. Wouldn't want to leave that necessity behind. My child is nearly eighteen months old, and that sanitizer is still 95 percent full on her dresser, by the way.

When we left the hospital, I felt the same way I do when I'm sneaking a four-course meal into a movie theater: trying so hard to act nonchalant that I'm actually drawing attention to myself with my awkwardness. "Nothing to see here, folks, just some people leaving a hospital with four pieces of luggage, nothing weird at all going on here! Did we drop something? Don't look back! Don't look back! It's gone, keep moving, save the rest!"

When I presented what Becky and I had done to the MOFLs, I was worried that perhaps I was the only mother who marked her child's birth with grand larceny, but I was relieved to find out quite a few of us have questionable morals. This could be the entire reason for the health-care crisis, now that I think about it. At the time I actually worried that we might get a bill for all the items we took, similar to the $15.95 hotel charges you see upon checkout if you've moved anything in the minifridge.

When discussing hospital loot we all agreed that the number-one grab needs to be the little nose sucker thing they use. For some reason the hospital ones work about 576 times better than the ones you'll buy at the store. But seeing as the ones from the store don't work *at all*, I guess that's not a really tough race to win. Do yourself a favor and snag as many of those as you can get your hands on. They have a way of getting lost (some may call this karma) or eaten by animals (even if you are not raising your child in the wild). Until your child understands the concept of blowing his or her nose, that sucky thing will prove quite helpful in sucking out the roughly forty-five tons of snot that your child will produce in his or her first years of life.

Beyond that, the list of grabbable items is long and varied:

Diaper bag: Sometimes the hospital is nice enough to actually provide you with a very cheap diaper bag. I'm not sure if their intention is for you to fill it with all their supplies, but let's go with yes.

Blankets: The "blankets" they use at the hospital are usually more like thick sheets. They are nothing fancy, but for some reason they are often the key to swaddling success. Grab as many as you can. Babies lay waste to everything in the first few months, so it's important to have backups handy.

Pacifiers: This is a taste thing—some kids like pacifiers, some like only a certain type, some can't be pacified by anything. If your kid likes the hospital binkies, try to grab three hundred. I had been warned repeatedly not to let the baby even see a pacifier, because she wouldn't want my boob afterward, so I kept her away from pacifiers in the hospital. I somehow think that she would prefer my boob either way, seeing as it shot food out of it and didn't keep falling out of her mouth every time she moved—but what do I know?

Diapers: Always take diapers wherever they are offered, end of story. Don't ask questions; just load up.

Hats: Cute baby hats? Three please.

Lotion / hand sanitizer: In our post-pandemic world it never hurts to grab a gallon or two of hand sanitizer whenever it is offered.

Bed pad protector things: These are the things that they put under your butt/back in bed to keep your uterus from destroying the sheets during what Chipper Jen calls your "crime scene" time during and post-birth. I feel like that is a perfect description of what is going on. Grab as many of these as you can. Your mattress will thank you for it later.

Disposable underwear: Following the pushing of the watermelon from your nether regions, putting on regular formfitting underwear is not really an option, so these bad boys take their place.

These are also lovely if you have been cut open for a C-section and can't stand anything tight on your poor belly. They are mesh, so as not to fit too snugly, and soft for comfort. The ones I got were half-way between underwear and shorts. Grab bunches. Amy, mother of two, is a big fan of these things: "The BEST. Sometimes I still sleep in them because they are so comfy." She tries, however, not to wear them to work, as they leave a very unfortunate panty line.

Maxi pads / adult diapers: Because of the "crime scene" time you'll experience (whether you deliver vaginally or via C-section), you will be provided with what are referred to as maxi pads. However, given the sheer size (think flotation device), these should be called adult diapers. Take as many packages of these as they will give you, and get used to sitting on what feels like a pillow between your legs.

Dermoplast / lady-parts spray bottle: I hate to dwell on such a (literally) sensitive spot, but the whooha needs to be well attended to post–hospital stay. No one wants to go to the store to buy Dermoplast (whooha numbing spray), and no one wants to try to figure out the cleaning situation without the Lady-Part Spray Bottle (put water in, spray to clean up instead of using toilet paper). Trust me. Grab all these things, and you will be fully equipped to handle your business in peace.

Flat-screen TV: Hey, it doesn't hurt to try . . .

4

BREASTFEEDING IS REALLY F'N HARD

(your nipples will never
know what hit them)

Two products with labels telling you not to use them:

1. Cigarettes

2. Baby formula (no pressure though . . .)

Random places my MOFLS have nursed:

Chipper Jen: In the bathroom of a pizza joint! I forgot my cover so I had to put my foot up on the toilet in the stall and lay the baby on my thigh with her feet dangling off and I was all bent over! Super awkward!

Sarah: I've nursed in dressing rooms, backseats of cars, restaurants, Disneyland, boats, etc.!

Erika: McDonald's . . . while scarfing McNuggets. Weak road trip moment.

Salpy: Oh, anywhere! In a bathroom, in church, in my kid's classroom, while walking around Target the other day.

Jenine: Yep, everywhere! And my daughter thinks those pretty covers are for hide-and-seek, so I've given up on them. Now I just try to hold my shirt over her a little and pretend her head covers me anyway.

Amy: I nursed my daughter on an airplane. She was the LOUDEST eater and would snort the whole time. Lucky for me I was sitting next to two men . . . not awkward at all.

B reastfeeding is the most natural thing on the planet. A connection between a mother and her offspring. The gift of food and life and love and—holy hell—is that a blister ON THE TIP OF MY NIPPLE???!!!

So yeah, despite the claims of every baby book, blog, doctor, midwife, woman, and some men (who always seem to be fans of anything having to do with boobs), it turns out that breastfeeding is actually really f'n hard. Before I go any further, is there a chance that your baby will pop out and land square on your boob, latch perfectly, and nourish itself with no problems whatsoever? Yes, of course (and yes, of course I will want to slap you as a result), but I believe there needs to be a very real shift in expectations among pregnant women when it comes to their breastfeeding capabilities.

As it stands now, we are all told that breastfeeding is the ONLY option for feeding your child, *if* you actually love that child and ever want them to have more than a third-grade level reading ability. If you don't breastfeed your baby, you might as well just drop it off immediately at your local prison, because that is where it's going to end up anyway, with such a horrible start to its life. Breastfeeding is beautiful and natural and the best and only socially acceptable way to nourish your baby. It is the most natural thing on the planet, you see.

Fast-forward to a severely sleep-deprived, hormone-riddled new mom whose baby is not latching on correctly. If maybe perhaps she had been warned that breastfeeding would not necessarily be easy-peasy, then maybe perhaps she wouldn't have to add "severe guilt" and "feelings of extreme failure as a woman and mother" to her already long list of postpartum difficulties.

So say it with me now: "Breastfeeding is really f'n hard." Repeat it to yourself, even as you attend classes and read books. Go into your feeding attempts knowing that it might not click right away, it might hurt like hell, your nipples may stretch to lengths that seem Guinness World Record–ish. But don't worry! That's all normal! Nature is a cruel, cruel bitch.

When my daughter first came out, I had her on my boob within a couple of minutes. A nice nurse came over and grabbed the baby, grabbed my boob, and forced the two together. Unfortunately, that nurse was unable to do this for me every time I fed the baby (I know, because I asked), so I began to have trouble. I thought I was latching the baby correctly, and I knew she was sucking like crazy; what more could possibly be needed for this equation? My nipples hurt LIKE HELL, but I thought that was just how this motherhood thing was going to go. After all, I burst onto the scene with an un- wanted drug-free delivery (the drug-free part, not the delivery). So, pain seemed to be my new normal. The nurses would ask me if ev- erything was going okay with the breastfeeding, and I would say yes. And they would just take my word for it. Because of course I knew what the hell I was talking about, right?

Shockingly, despite my very educated and experienced procla- mations, the baby wasn't actually feeding on me correctly, which was made apparent by her drastic weight loss in her first hours of life. This led to quite a few more nurses grabbing my boob and the baby and putting the two together.

It also warranted a visit from the Very Serious Lactation Con- sultant. This woman is all boob, all the time. When you say the words "bottle" or "pacifier" to this woman, she looks at you like you just said, "light the baby on fire." When my Very Serious Lactation

Consultant arrived in the room, I asked her to please teach me how to feed my baby in a way that (1) actually fed my baby and (2) helped my aching nipples remain on my body for at least another forty-eight to seventy-two hours. VSLC said she could help and quickly reclined my hospital bed. Then she opened my shirt and placed the baby face down on my belly.

"It's totally natural; she will crawl right up and find your breast and eat."

Seeing as the child was only a day old, I had my doubts about her climbing abilities, but this setup was just random enough for me to remain interested. And what do you know—that little baby slowly started making her way up my belly, to my breast. I had to guide her a bit so she didn't fall off onto the bed, but together we got her up there. The Very Serious Lactation Consultant smiled widely, as if her work here was done.

"Um, yeah, so that was super interesting in a *National Geographic* sort of way, but I don't think it's going to be all that practical for me to disrobe and lie down on my back every time I need to feed the baby. First of all, it might get awkward when I'm out at a restaurant, and second, I feel like making the baby run a little baby marathon before she gets to eat is sorta mean."

Hmph. My VSLC didn't really enjoy my lack of enthusiasm for her "Climb Every Mammary" technique, but she did eventually move on to teaching me some other backup options, should I not be able to find a nice place to lie on the floor *every* time the child needed to eat.

While her other techniques were a little more practical, they weren't without their challenges. For instance, they actually required the assistance of a very awkwardly positioned assistant to join baby and boob correctly. Awesome. I feel like when an activity requires reinforcement staff and an elaborate pulley system, it might not actually be "the most natural thing on the planet." But I pressed on.

Even after I got a handle on the latching, my baby was still a little underweight because, oh, didn't anyone mention? Your milk can take a while to actually come in. Nature is fun like that. The poor kid can be sucking like crazy and getting colostrum (pre-milk healthy goodness), but they're not getting the milk yet—and maybe not even getting a ton of colostrum. So, after I fed her, I also had to pump and try to get some milk to supplement her. The nurses wanted to supplement her with formula, but the Very Serious Lactation Consultant made it very clear that if I were to allow my baby to (1) drink from a bottle or (2) drink formula, the world would come crashing down—and I was barely holding it up as it was.

So I would pump my poor sore boobs for an hour and get *juuuust* enough to fill a needleless syringe with milk. How do you know that you haven't pumped a lot? When an eyedropper can pick up all the milk you've just expressed. Shockingly, even after that feast the baby was still hungry. So, through hysterical tears (again, par for my new course; see Chapter 7, "So Many Tears") I allowed Vivian to be supplemented with a little formula between breastfeeding sessions, to get her weight up. I felt like a complete maternal failure, and she wasn't even forty-eight hours old. I was really hoping to put off that feeling until she made an unfortunate piercing choice in her teen years.

On top of this, Vivian had tummy issues from day one—issues that it took me a few hard weeks to realize were alleviated when I stopped eating ALL dairy (always start with cutting out dairy if the baby has belly issues). And beans. And anything spicy. So in addition to the caffeine I had given up as soon as I found out I was pregnant, I was now living a dairy-free (and nacho-free) life. Silver lining: I did lose my baby weight pretty quickly when I lost the ability to eat cheese, soda, and nachos. So there's that.

Then, once I thought I had breastfeeding figured out, my milk would still occasionally dip in production. For no real reason my boobs would slow down, and I was convinced this meant I was drying up. Images of ice cream would start dancing in my head, but then I read online that sometimes this happens, and that I shouldn't give up. Dammit, I had to cancel my large pizza. I would pump after every feeding, trying to convince my boobs that I suddenly had twins who were very, very hungry. This usually got us back on track pretty quickly.

But even after I learned how to weather the ups and downs in my production, and cheese had become a distant memory in my pizza-topping past, I still found the whole thing to be a lot of responsibility. I had to think twice about every single thing I consumed. I had to plan my days around feeding, pumping, and storing. Going out of town without the kid for even a night was difficult for me and the baby. Overall, it is very weird, beautiful, and somewhat overwhelming to know that your body is responsible for another life. Between pregnancy and breastfeeding my body was Vivian's for almost two years. And that's the gig. But it's still a lot of responsibility.

When Vivian was around ten months old, she caught a violent flu bug that was spread to several kids at a playdate from hell. The result was that she would feed on me, sit up, and promptly projectile vomit her meal all over both of us. I tried to feed her for less time to limit the projected amount, but then she was losing out on the snuggling that she loved so much and would be in hysterics when I cut her off. This went on for a few days, and I finally hit my breaking point. I moved her over to bottles full time so that I could gauge how much she was actually eating and not traumatize both of us post–nipple removal. Could I have weathered that storm and kept feeding? Probably. But for some reason that moment was my final straw. (It's a possibility that the reason might have had something to do with the plate of nachos and extra-large Mountain Dew I consumed for my first post-breastfeeding meal. Sorry Vivi, Mommy was hungry.)

I felt so guilty when I stopped breastfeeding, as if I had failed my daughter by not making it to my goal of a year. I was also a little sad that I no longer had that special time with her, those calm minutes with just the two of us holding each other close. I missed it. But my boobs missed it even more. Unaware that the milk train had been taken off the tracks, my champion breasts continued to produce with vigor. They looked like two water balloons that could burst at any second, the idea of which seemed very gross but also like it might not feel very good, because the pressure was awful. I called the advice nurse, because I was pretty sure no one had ever experienced anything like this before, and if they had, surely the medical community had devised a way to alleviate it. Helpful Advice Nurse said, "Yeah, that really hurts. It'll eventually go away, though." Thanks, so helpful.

I was told that if I relieved the pressure by pumping, the boobs would take that to mean I was still feeding and would continue making the milk I was trying to dry up. So, I would let my boobs get full enough—to the point where I honestly thought an explosion was a possibility—and then I would pump a little tiny bit to relieve the pain and pressure. I read that putting cabbage on your boobs helps, so I put an entire salad bar on them. Then I was in pain *and* had wilted produce falling off me. It's all so glamorous I could slap somebody.

When I look back on it now, the entire breastfeeding saga didn't actually last that long in the grand scheme of things, and if I'm being honest, breastfeeding is where I was forced to learn how to be a mom. In the beginning, my partner was much better at all things baby, so I was quick to hand Vivian off because I felt inadequate most of the time. She had a wobbly head that scared me, and diaper changes were not my strong suit. But being the owner of the magic boobs meant there was no option for handing the baby over for feedings—I had to figure it out. Vivian and I struggled at first, but every two to three hours we'd come together and do our best to get her fed. When we were successful, she would fall asleep in my arms after eating, and I would recline the chair to snooze as well. Then she'd wake up, I'd perch her up on my legs and I'd talk to her while she kicked and cooed. She couldn't talk back, but it was during those endless hours that we got to know each other. I got to know her laugh and her rhythms. I mastered changing diapers and how to not drop a slippery baby. It was hard to recognize at the time, but our breastfeeding experience was one of the best things to happen to me as a new mom who needed to figure out how to operate a baby.

But, like everything else during the first year of parenting, breastfeeding and its difficulties seemed endless when they were happening. As though it were a possibility that I would be whipping a boob out in restaurants for years to come. When I had blisters on my nipples but still had to let the baby nurse, when I had to pump and dump because I accidently ate some ranch dressing at dinner, when I would have to watch my boobs being violently and rhythmically sucked into the breast pump—all these things were intense during an already overwhelming time, and they came with the inevitable feeling that there was no end in sight.

Despite how hard it is, I am not trying to talk anyone out of breastfeeding. (I believe a gaggle of angry lactation consultants would violently swarm my house if I were to suggest such a thing—and they are unnaturally strong from having to wrestle unwilling boobs all day.) What I'm trying to do is prepare you for the fact that it might not be easy-peasy. As one of my MOFLs said, "The breastfeeding class I took failed to mention cracked nipples, excruciating pain, clogged ducts, and mastitis." If you go into breastfeeding knowing that it could be difficult, then you may be less likely to quit in a fit of shame/frustration/inferiority when you hit those really common speed bumps.

So ladies, breastfeed your babies, and don't stop if it gets a little tough. And don't be afraid to talk about the fact that it's tough. There is no shame whatsoever in struggling with absolutely anything having to do with your efforts to keep your little person alive. But also, if it gets way too tough, or things don't work out, or you just don't want to do it—don't beat yourself up about it. Your kid will be fine.

Just because breastfeeding is natural doesn't mean it will come naturally to you right off the bat. Find someone supportive (a friend, a mom, a doctor) you can talk to if you are having trouble or doubts. Go to the lactation clinic every damn day if you need to. You are not a failure as a woman or mother if breastfeeding is hard. What you are is a sleep-deprived, overwhelmed, hormone-riddled woman who, for some reason, has been trusted with caring for a newborn. Nature needs to get that timing thing worked out a little better, if you ask me.

I'm not really sure why the challenges of breastfeeding aren't spoken about more often. It's a shame, because nothing is worse than feeling as if you are the only mom who has ever struggled. Every time I bring it up around moms, pretty much everyone has a horror story to tell, so why aren't these stories more readily shared? Let's share some now, shall we?

Sarah agrees, "It was definitely harder and much more painful, in the beginning, than anyone mentioned."

Dana explains, "My first was definitely more difficult. She didn't really grasp the sucking thing and was a little lazy. It took us a couple months to really figure it out. I ended up weaning her around six months. It was very physically and emotionally draining at times. And I have to say I was in no way prepared for it to be challenging. Everything I read made it sound like these babies had already gone through breastfeeding school in the womb and would know exactly what to do."

A couple of moms had so much trouble with breastfeeding that they had to stop early on. Chipper Jen was not so chipper when her first child refused to latch correctly. "I did breastfeed Maddyn [second child] until she was fourteen months old. And I got crap for breastfeeding that long from some people. Austin [first child] was a totally different story. I struggled for three months, trying anything and everything to get him to breastfeed because that's what everybody said I needed to do. I hired lactation consultants, rented a hospital-grade pump, used nipple shields, and even resorted to taking some kind of herbal supplement to increase my milk flow. Turns out, he was lazy and just didn't want to latch, and when he did, he tore me up. But I beat myself up for three months because I felt like the worst mom ever. We switched to formula when he was three months old, and he is just as healthy as my daughter."

Sommer lived far away from her family and friends when her baby was born. And her husband's job took him away right after the baby arrived. This left a very stressed-out mom to battle through postpartum issues alone. Sommer says, "My milk just didn't come in (probably based on my stress level at the time). I was prepared that breastfeeding may be hard, but I had no idea that women would be so judgmental of one another."

Both Jen and Sommer touched on the judgment that many women feel no matter what their breastfeeding choice ends up being. It's a unique slap in your already-bruised face when a fellow mom raises her eyebrow at how you choose to feed your baby. As if you have been pregnant and new-mothering in a vacuum that does not include any information on anything relating to the best care for an infant and were just waiting for someone to enlighten you with their all-knowingness. What on earth would I do without your judgmental sighs and sideways glances, Perfect Mom?

Michelle tries to counter those moms. "I am fully supportive of all ways a mom chooses to feed her child, and hope to help ease some of the frustration, because a mother's sanity is the most important thing."

And don't worry—even if breastfeeding is going great, you can still get a glaring eye. Amy explains how you can't win: "Unlike other women, my in-laws and friends did NOT breastfeed their babies. So I always felt like the hippie mom, the granola mom, always having to head to a back room at the most inconvenient times to pull out the boob rather than pull out a convenient bottle. And then, of course, there are people who think it's weird and disgusting if a mom continues breastfeeding after one year."

So you see, it's bound to be tons of fun, no matter what you do.

PARTNER CORNER: BREASTFEEDING

Jason: A HUGE tip . . . I'd heard from someone about a lactation consultant. When my wife had trouble producing milk on day two, I called a lactation consultant, paid the $100, and it changed EVERYTHING. My wife was able to feed him, and it was one of the most important things we did for his health.

Pat: My partner didn't really have the best of luck breastfeeding. She didn't produce enough milk, so we had to use formula and because of that, we switched feedings between the two of us, which helped. I think if you can rotate who feeds, especially with a bottle, it's important for the dad to be involved. It helps with the bonding part.

Tom: Making sure she was as comfortable as possible and had everything she needed so she wouldn't have to get up and interrupt the process. This was a tad self-serving as well, because once feeding started and there was nothing more for me to do, that meant sleep for me.

Larry: My only job outside of a few daily bottle feedings was to organize and properly store stock. A job I did so well you'd have thunk I worked on a dairy farm. Also, I know men have read that gentle boob massage can help with lactation. That seems to be the only breastfeeding tip we manage to remember. Some advice: don't be the one to bring it up or offer this to your partner. Trust me, she is well aware of your motives and obsessions.

5

THEY WILL LET YOU TAKE A BABY HOME!

(in fact, they encourage it)

Things I was qualified to do pre-baby:

- Juggle
- Text, email, surf the web, play games, and check my bank balance on my phone, one handed
- Drive a car (but parallel parking is not my strong suit)
- Type seventy words per minute
- Find, book, and be on a vacation in less than two days
- Sleep through just about anything
- Movie-hop to five movies in one day
- Find a new restaurant to eat at every single night

Things I actually do post-baby:

- Take care of an infant
- Text, email, surf the web, play games, and check my bank balance on my phone, one handed

Even after fortyish weeks of pregnancy, excruciating labor, and your time at the hospital post-baby, you will still be at least a bit surprised when health-care professionals allow you to take your newborn home with you. This is a very frightening reality, one that you really hoped to be better prepared for.

Throughout my fortyish weeks of pregnancy, I kept assuming (i.e., hoping) that as soon as the baby actually arrived something would just click inside of me, and all of a sudden I would know how to parent a newborn. Seeing as I don't even really like babies, I should have realized that a simple click was unlikely. When the click wasn't clicking in the first couple of days, I began to panic a bit. When it was officially time to leave the hospital, I freaked the hell out.

Somehow I knew that no matter how much stuff I stole from the hospital, I still wasn't going to miraculously know what to do with a little baby once I got home. And no matter what I crammed into my bag, it seemed impossible to fit what I really wanted to bring home: the nurses. Throughout my time in the hospital, I asked the nurses roughly 7,232 questions a day and went running to the nurses' station at least twice a night because I had no idea what to do with this very little person (who, in my defense, would periodically choke and stop breathing—hence the running). The thought of going home without someone with a degree in medicine was an extremely daunting one.

I often thought that night nurses looking for work should stand outside the birthing center every day like day laborers stand outside the Home Depot. As parents are sent home with their new merchandise, nothing would be more appealing than taking home a real-life reference manual as well. Those women could be millionaires within two weeks. Freaked-out new parents would pay a high premium for help. I know I would have picked up at least two.

My advice for taking home the nurses (besides an elaborate kidnapping scheme that you will simply not have the energy to execute) is to absorb as much of their knowledge as possible prior to leaving the hospital. When you are in the hospital around the clock, you will go through four shifts of nurses (and unfortunately you will be awake to meet all of them). In my case, these shifts brought in quite a diversity of women, ranging in age, ethnicity, experience, and opinion. The thing I enjoyed most about these different women was their sometimes–polar opposite answers to the questions I asked. I liked that the health-care provider had clearly not given their nurses a "party line" to spew out for each standard question I'm sure they are asked roughly four hundred times a day. Their answers seemed to be a result of their own experiences and, in many cases, their age.

So I just kept asking questions, sometimes the same question to each of the nurses, and kept storing away their answers in my mind (back when my mind was still a viable storage option). One of the most fantastic aspects of trying to decipher a baby is that it turns out they are all different, just like real people. So it's always a good idea to have plenty of answers stored up when a question presents itself, because odds are the first few won't work, and even if they do work, it might not work the next time. Real people are a pain like that.

The first night we were home from the hospital, I was a mess of nerves and sleep deprivation, convinced that something horrible was going to happen with no nurses outside the door to help. Then, in the middle of a breastfeeding session, stormy weather knocked the power out. This did not help my panic—at all. We set up candles around the house to complete the *Little House on the Prairie* look I was so hoping to replicate on my first night home with a new baby. I had visions of the power being out for days, us freezing inside with no heater, the child developing hypothermia.

The power came back on ten minutes later, juuuust before we all lost toes from frostbite. It was a trying time, to be sure. Mommy's first mental breakdown. Mark it down in the baby book.

It seems I may be in the minority in thinking I was completely unqualified to take a baby home from the hospital. My MOFLs had a little more confidence in their abilities than I did. Although we all implemented the age-old, highly technical "check for breathing every five seconds" method of ensuring the newborn's survival.

Chipper Jen volunteers, "I'm pretty sure I didn't put Austin down until I absolutely had to! I woke up with every movement, noise, cough, etc., and then when he DIDN'T move or make noise I was checking him to see if he was breathing!"

When asked about her first night, Amy said, "We were so overly confident our first night. All systems were go until she started screaming, and screaming, and screaming... and she wouldn't stop. We tried everything and nothing would soothe her. Then we realized she was gassy and we had no medicine. So my husband went to the store at 2:00 a.m. to get her Mylicon, and she eventually calmed down." This is another shocking new baby discovery: They cry. A lot.

Sommer did make me feel a little better about my own struggles. "Kash is now a year old. . . . I'm finally figuring this mommy thing out!!"

I asked Carrie whether she was freaked out the first night home and how long it took her to actually feel like she knew what she was doing. Her answer is super-reassuring, too. "Not sure I was freaking out (not really my style), but I'm pretty sure I still don't know what I'm doing, and now I have two!" If that doesn't inspire confidence in your upcoming years and months, I don't know what will.

The main thing to remember is that no, you have no idea what you are doing, but thankfully your baby doesn't know any better, and frankly they don't have a lot of other options anyway. So take a deep breath and settle in for a wild ride. And pray the electricity stays on.

PARTNER CORNER: EARLY DAYS

Pat: You will need to find help locally. If you don't have parents close by, you are doomed. Sorry, but it's true. My best advice is to go to the supermarket by your house, set up a table like the Girl Scouts, and recruit some nannies or old people who will act like your parents. Because you will need someone to help.

Tom: As the dad (with no paternity time off available), it felt like I was missing out a lot—not just on being there for the baby, but also with being able to relieve my wife and "tag in" as much as I wish I could have. It felt like there was this air of "well, she's the mom, she stays home and takes care of the baby, and you go to work." It feels like we still need to make some advances when it comes to that kind of thinking.

6

YOU ARE GOING TO NEED SOME BACKUP

'm sure you've heard the phrase, "It takes a village to raise a child." I'm not sure about the entire raising of a child, because I've only just recently gotten mine upright, but I do know that for the first few months you are definitely going to need villagers. However, you need to find a unique village that houses only women, and only women who have experience with babies. You really have no use for the rest of the village.

Even if you have nannied since you were six years old and grew up in a family of ten, you are still going to need help the first few weeks and months (possibly years?) of your child's life. It's an exhausting and emotional time, and the more support you have, the better. I recommend you find as many women who know what to do with babies as you can. Then I recommend inviting them all over to hold your baby while you nap or take a shower (or nap in the shower).

If you are married, I sincerely hope your spouse, like mine, is a woman who has taken care of many babies. But if for some reason you weren't able to arrange that, then it is very likely that your partner has even less of an idea what to do with a baby than you do. He will probably want to help as much as he can, but he will most likely lack the skills or confidence to really take over when you need a break. That is not to say that men are useless, or that you should allow them to be useless simply because they may look like Big Foot holding a complicated remote control when they cradle their new baby. Most men want to help—it's in their DNA. The problem is that they also really want to not break the baby, and breaking feels like a very real possibility when attempting to handle such a wobbly little thing. So, they are often frozen by lack of experience and fear of failure.

The only solution is to make sure your partner is attending the same Baby Care 101 crash course you are, which means keeping them involved and not allowing helpers to push them aside. He or she needs to bond with the baby and should not get out of participating because of lack of experience. None of us really have any idea what we are doing with our first child, but somehow we figure it out. Your partner will be in for a very rude awakening when your helpers stop helping if he or she hasn't been learning from day one.

Make sure you talk to your partner before the baby arrives and try to hammer out an agreement on how you will tag-team the "keeping the baby alive" task before you. Everything won't go exactly as you plan, but it will be good to at least have an understanding between the two of you before the chaos begins. I know quite a few dads who have handled the majority of the diaper changes because mom is doing the breastfeeding. Tell your partner that if they commit to the diaper task, they will earn fifty katrillion Good Partner Points, which instantly get redeemed for New Mom Love and jealousy from every other mom on the planet who hears the tale.

Also, make sure you set your boundaries with any helpers you have signed up. Most will tread lightly and be very conscious of not stepping on any toes, but the occasional (ahem, overbearing mother-in-law, ahem) helper can take your inexperience as a sign to simply take over, and maybe not in the way you prefer. They will do this with the best of intentions (keeping the baby alive), but it's best if you talk to all your helpers in advance and let them know that no matter how useless you may seem in your post-baby haze, you have certain preferences when it comes to taking care of your baby. Try to communicate those preferences, maybe even jot them down in advance.

Basically, try to do as much planning in advance as you can, because after the baby arrives your brain will slowly turn to mush and leave you unable and unwilling to put up much of a fight about anything. And you shouldn't have to. The people who offer to help you after your new baby arrives really do want to help in any way you deem fit. Do not hesitate to ask them for anything you need those first few days as you get your bearings, and let them know constantly how grateful you are for their help.

As I mentioned, I was lucky enough to have a partner who had quite a bit of experience with babies, so I was able to count on her to take over when I was feeling inadequate or overwhelmed (a.k.a. 95 percent of the time). I also had my mom and my aunt, who stopped by to lend a hand for the first few weeks. They were such lifesavers because I couldn't rest or take my eyes off the baby if I didn't feel like someone was watching over her. Even when she was sleeping at night, I would constantly check to make sure she was okay, so there wasn't much "sleep while the baby sleeps" happening.

Having experienced hands on deck meant that I could confidently go lie down for a couple hours and get some solid rest without worrying that I was sleeping through one of the 1,400 possible crisis situations I had read about on the internet. In the beginning, that rest was the most valuable thing any helper could give me. It didn't hurt that they also brought homemade meals and calming energy, both of which were in very short supply those first few weeks.

Pretty much all my MOFLs said that their moms came to help out for at least the first couple of weeks their new baby was home. Moms are great because they are equally in love with your new baby, you know they have history of keeping babies alive (you), and sometimes their presence alone makes you feel a little calmer. Also, they often bring snacks.

Monica, mom of four, found a tremendous support system in her church: "I have had endless help from the relief society women in my church. Meals for three weeks straight. Drop-ins to help clean my house or just hold the crying baby for me. A couple of them took over picking up my kids from school. Truly a humbling experience. I know some people think us Mormons are kinda crazy, but I've never felt so much help and love than I have from those women!!!"

Sommer, mom of one, was away from a big portion of her family and friends when she had her son, so she took other measures to ensure help. "I hired a doula. Thank god!!! But I also developed a network of new momma friends. We became close during our pregnancies and then stayed close after we had our babies. That was crucial for me! It is SO important to have a support system!"

Sommer touches on another group of people you should line up in advance: women who have or have had young children to answer your ridiculous baby questions and provide general moral support. Yes, your mom will do a great job with the new baby, but it's also a good idea to have some women on call who have recent newborn experience. I can barely remember what I did last week, so by the time my daughter is grown and asking me for advice on her own babies, I'm going to be quite useless.

I was lucky enough to have a few friends who were very patient with my endless stream of panic texts about every mundane baby matter. Most of the panic was a result of ill-advised internet searches (see Chapter 17, "Who Needs a Health Plan When You Have the Internet?" [which I knew were a bad idea, but which I did anyway]). My friends were kind enough to keep reassuring me that my kid was going to be okay—and keep reminding me that deep-diving on the internet was not the most productive way to spend my time.

All this talk about how much help you are going to need should not scare you into thinking that you will be completely useless when it comes to your new baby. The fact is, you will be fine. You'll figure it out, you'll get the hang of it, and eventually you will be the old pro that other moms are texting for advice. But it never hurts to have support from friends and family when tackling such a big life change. It's not often that people offer to come over to your house, do chores for you, give you meals, and generally be at your beck and call. I say embrace it—and try to convince them to stay through the teenage years, if at all possible.

PARTNER CORNER: KEEPING IT 50/50

Larry: It would help to realize it will NEVER be 50/50 with a baby. Men can't lactate, and babies spend an eternity on the boob. I would suggest becoming a deliberate empath (I made that up), as I did. On my way home I'd imagine my wife trapped at home with a parasite attached to her boob all day. That would give me the motivation to come in and save her, even if I was tired myself. I wasn't always happy carrying my children around while tired after a long day of work, but with the aid of a good carrier and being honest about what I was feeling, it worked out for me and ultimately us.

Tom: If you think, "Well, she changed a diaper, and I changed a diaper, so we're even," you need to recalibrate. She pushed a human out of her body, a baby which is now clamping down on her to feed several times a day. So however you help out, things will never even out. Go above and beyond as much as you can when it comes to duties that both of you can do.

Jason: Literally just show up. Ask what she needs. Shut up and do it. It will NEVER be 50 percent; you can't breastfeed at night. And someone needs to work (me, in this case). So, I just did what I could. Oh, and tell her how much you appreciate all that she's doing, and acknowledge that you know her job is the harder one.

7

SO MANY TEARS

(and some from the baby, too)

Things that made you cry pre-baby	vs.	Things that make you cry post-baby
Sad commercials		Everything (especially stubbing your toe)
Stubbing your toe		

Things that cheered you up pre-baby	vs.	Things that cheer you up post-baby
A good laugh		A nap
A good hug		When your baby has gas, but looks like they are smiling
A good talk		

When I thought of postpartum depression before I had a baby, I thought of women losing their minds and doing crazy things to themselves or their children. Although I knew it was a common condition for new mothers, the only real stories I'd heard about it were the maternal snaps that made headlines. I didn't foresee throwing my baby across the room, so in some ways I shrugged off the possibility of postpartum depression. However, I've definitely dealt with depression throughout my life, so I knew there was a possibility it would crop up after the new baby arrived. Somehow, though, part of me believed that if I remained aware of my inclination, I could talk myself out of the baby blues.

Smash cut to me crying hysterically for no apparent reason while holding my newborn. A blubbering mess from a woman who was devoid of most human emotions pre-baby. Everyone who knew me pre-baby was alarmed, to say the least.

There are different levels of postpartum sadness, ranging from what is classified as "baby blues," to "postpartum depression," and up to "postpartum psychosis." Chances are you will fall into one of the first two categories at some point shortly after giving birth. (It's just nonstop excitement, isn't it?!)

There are a lot of factors that may make you more susceptible to postpartum depression, but it's hard to predict exactly how your brain and body will respond to having a baby. And although you hopefully will have left the hospital with a bag full of industrial-strength maxi pads to help with whatever's going on with your body (see Chapter 3), your brain is a different story. First, there are the changes in your hormone levels after childbirth. Then there is sleep deprivation (please see Chapter 18, "You'll Never Sleep Again") and the fact that your entire world has just been turned upside down (please see Chapter 12, "Your Life Is Officially Over"). Mix all this together, and you really have a cocktail for good times.

Baby blues and postpartum depression have similar symptoms: moodiness, crying, irritability, sadness, trouble sleeping, and feelings of guilt or worthlessness. The difference between a case of the baby blues and a more serious depression is the intensity of your symptoms and how long they last. Baby blues last from only a few days to a couple of weeks. Postpartum depression can linger for months. Ultimately, if left untreated, full-on depression can interfere with your ability to take care of yourself and the baby.

The best thing to do if you are feeling a little or a lot upset is to talk to someone you trust and always, always be honest with your health-care provider, so they can help you in the best medical ways available. Do not feel ashamed or like less of a mother if you have depression issues. Your body is a mess, you aren't sleeping, and everything is ass over teakettle. You are entitled to some tears. And to some help. You are not weak; you are healing. Allow yourself to.

Talk to your partner before the baby arrives. Let him or her know that postpartum depression is very real and could affect you. Often spouses feel just as helpless as the new mom when she goes off to a dark place. Tell your partner to read up on it online in advance, to talk to your doctor about it if it arises, and most important, to know that they can't "fix" it. It will be their instinct to want to help you when you are crying or hurt, to figure out a way to stop the tears, but it's just not a possibility when it comes to baby blues. This can be very frustrating and scary for your partner, especially if they are not aware of the possibility before it arises.

After a couple of days of me having breakdowns, Becky finally stopped asking what was wrong and just starting saying, "Are we gonna have our cry now?" I would nod and start welling up. This, of course, wasn't a long-term solution, but for me it was nice to know that I could be a heap of tears without having to explain it or her trying to fix it. It just was, and then eventually it stopped, even though it felt like it was going to last forever.

My friends were quietly supportive, too, understanding when I didn't want visitors and not pushing me when it was clear that I needed some time to gather myself. One friend even did a drive-by meal drop-off while I hid away in the nursery with the baby. She was in and out in a couple of minutes, didn't ask questions or push to see the newborn. As for taking care of myself, I didn't say yes if I wanted to say no, I didn't push myself to be overly happy if I felt not so sunshiny. I forced myself to get out of the house and go for walks. I gave myself time to be sad and hoped like hell it would pass. And it did.

Of course, this is not the case for everyone, and sometimes you will need more than just time and an understanding support system to get through your postpartum issues. This is why being honest with your doctor at follow-up appointments is important. He or she will be able to determine whether you may need additional help.

I wanted to discuss postpartum depression and baby blues a little bit not to give you a completely thorough understanding of the causes and treatment, but to make you aware that it is very, very common and a very, very real possibility for your life post-delivery. Like so many parts of this parenting adventure, I feel like postpartum depression isn't discussed in a way that makes pregnant women *expect* that it will happen to them. Statistics say that

80 percent of women suffer from some form of baby blues or post-partum depression. Seeing as many women don't ever even talk about it, I would say that number is probably even higher.

The point is this: Even though you have been waiting months, years, or maybe what feels like your whole life for this new little baby to bless your world, that doesn't mean that everything following his or her arrival is going to be easy. Even in the best circumstances, women suffer from depression; it's chemical, not logical. I dreamt of my little one for years, was beyond ecstatic to find out she was coming, and was surrounded by more love and support than I could ever have asked for after she arrived. And yet, I was still a blubbering mess most of the day.

So be kind to yourself; don't beat yourself up for not feeling or looking anything like how you imagined your post-baby glow would go. Talk to your partner, your doctor, your friends, and your family. Feel free to break down in tears if you need to. Just know that this feeling will not last forever and that eventually you will regain your footing emotionally and physically.

My MOFLs had plenty of experience with the baby blues. Sarah says, "I called the first seven weeks with Drew the Dark Days. I remember going out on the deck and just crying because I didn't think I would ever sleep again. With the second baby I just had a lot of anger and not so much sadness. But it all passes."

Michelle sums it up nicely: "You will cry and have no idea why. It will be okay and the crying will go away eventually."

Dana describes her tiny bout of baby blues, including symptoms that are very common among new moms: "I don't know if I ever had postpartum depression, but I definitely had mood swings, cried for no reason, got easily frustrated, and had some resentment for my husband, whose life didn't seem to be too altered by the new member of our family (at least not the way mine was)."

However, another Sarah dealt with much more serious issues. "I had it with each of my babies, but I struggle with depression anyway. My OB knew to keep an eye out. By my third it hit HARD. Fortunately, talk therapy and antidepressants (safe while nursing) helped a ton." In addition to medication Sarah has day-to-day advice for working through the tough times: "Exercise, eating right, sticking to a schedule—all these things help. I think telling your OB beforehand if it's something you struggle with and being honest at postpartum appointments is really important."

Monica did tiny things to keep her spirits up. "I just had to force myself and the babies out of the house. Nearly every day. It helped a ton. Even if it was just to get my car washed. They need more drive-thrus for moms and kids."

And even our chipper one had the baby blues! "I definitely had it worse with my first. The whole 'hard time breastfeeding, no sleep, still look pregnant, pain in my hoo hoo, husband not experiencing any of this' was rough the first few weeks!" But don't despair; Jen found a way out of the darkness, and of course it involved working out. "Going back to the gym after week six helped tremendously for everyone!"

Since going to the gym only brings me closer to my dark place, it was not an option for me. I did find that getting out of the house helped, but mostly just strolls around the block with the baby. She loved being outdoors, and a walk was a good way to move and get out of the house without having to pack her and all her accessories up for a car ride.

Also, if a friend or family member stopped by and offered to help, I took them up on it. I didn't chitchat, I just handed them the baby and took a little while for myself. I'd rest, or if I was feeling especially adventurous, I'd occasionally shower like a normal human. Big time stuff. It's amazing what a good shower can do for your spirit, especially when followed by a face-plant into a pillow. In fact, that's an activity list worth exploring long after the baby blues pass. It'll come in especially handy during the toddler tantrum age. (In case you were wondering if the excitement ever stops, the answer is no. Yay parenthood!)

PARTNER CORNER: ADVICE ON DEALING WITH HORMONAL WOMEN

Jason: Run!! Seriously, there is no way you are ever going to win a hormonal-based argument. My tactic: shut the F up, tell her she's right, and let her come around to see it my way later. (Or not . . . but half the time she would come around, so just leave it alone.)

Pat: Hahaha. . . . If I had advice about this, I would be a rich man.

Larry: Don't. Yield, bow your head, and back away slowly. Never turn your back. Your instinct once you turn your back is to murmur something under your breath, and trust me—she will hear you. On a serious note, be aware of postpartum issues like depression or anxiety. There is a difference between being hormonal and these serious medical issues.

8

YOUR NEWBORN IS NOT CUTE

(not even a little)

What you think your newborn looks like:

- An angel
- A little baby doll
- Perfection on earth
- Just like you (probably even if you don't share DNA)
- Much better looking than any baby you've ever seen

What your newborn actually looks like:

- Puffy
- A little monkey that has been submerged in water for nine months
- Sorta scary
- Nothing like you (because you are not a little monkey who has been submerged in water for nine months)
- Unattractive, like every other baby you've ever seen

Things people say when they see your newborn (instead of "Wow! That baby is ugly!"):

- "Awww, a baby!"
- "Ten fingers and ten toes, good job!"
- "That one is going to be a heartbreaker some day!"
- "Look at all that hair!"

hate to break it to you, but I'm afraid someone has to. Your new-born is not cute. There, I said it. I know you will disagree, but you are wrong. Check back with me in six months and let me know if you still think those first pictures of your darling bundle of joy didn't actually look like a bundle of shriveled alien.

I've worked out a very useful equation to explain whether you will think a child is cute:

Newborn = Not So Cute
Newborn + Love = Cuteness

The basis of this complicated equation is this: the more you love a baby, the cuter you will think it is at any given time, *especially* when it is brand new. I was never a big fan of babies, and I always thought they were all sorts of not cute. Then my goddaughter was born. And I thought she was genuinely the cutest newborn I had ever seen. Then my baby was born and I thought she was gorgeous as well. Looking back on pictures of both of them, I realize that they really just looked like every other newborn on the planet. So why did I see something else at the time? Because my love for them triggered a switch in my brain that then passed on a signal to my eyes: "Cute baby. Baby is cute. Flood body with feelings of love. Make sure they are fed and cared for."

I would venture a guess that this is an actual setting in our brains, one to ensure the survival of the young. If they were crying, drooling, pooping, not sleeping, *and* unattractive, there might be some longevity issues for the human race.

It does not matter what ethnicity your child is; they will inevi-tably be unattractive when fresh out of the gate. My child was light skinned with tons of black hair. I thought she looked amazing. I look at pictures now and I realize she actually looked like a baby monkey. When I was born my parents thought my dark skin and dark hair were beautiful. But in reality I had a unibrow and looked like an eighty-year-old man.

Now that I think about it, most newborn photos look strikingly similar to photos of the elderly. Elderly who have lived very, very hard lives. If your child is Caucasian with light hair? He or she will look exactly like Benjamin Button did when he was born. The Benjamin Button look took hours of makeup and teams of special effects professionals. Your baby's look took nine months of swimming in your uterus.

I say all this not to make you feel bad or to endanger the human race by having mothers recognize their children's shortcomings. I say this so you will take it into consideration before posting 5,472 photos of Benjamin Button on your Facebook page. Please keep in mind that there are a select few people in the world who have your blinders on—and the rest of us have no defense against the onslaught of unfortunate baby photos. Your child has baby acne, cradle cap, puffy eyes, a nose as big as a grown person, and one strand of hair—on his forehead. The internet can take only so much of all that awesome, trust me.

The only acceptable pictures of newborns are the ones taken by a professional photographer who uses great lighting, a top-notch camera, advanced Photoshop skills, and extreme selectivity in picking acceptable photos. You can trust these photos because they are taken by someone who (1) doesn't love your baby and (2) will have a very short career if they produce only ugly baby pictures. The babies in professional portraits are softened and edited to within an inch of their lives—sorta like cover models—because it's never too early for children to learn about our superficial society. Better for that lesson to be taught via an airbrushed photo than a scary snapshot that inspires an unavoidable grimace on all who catch a glimpse. Pay these photographers whatever they are charging to come to your house and take flattering photos of your baby. Believe me, it is worth it not to cringe at the sight of your child's newborn picture years from now.

Now, I know what you are thinking: "Everyone said Junior was adorable—they all fawned over him!" To which I respond with one of two things: either they love Junior just like you do, or, and this is more likely, they are lying. You are a heap of emotions who has literally just been torn open in your selfless efforts to bring new life into the world. No one is going to tell you that you spent nine months carrying and several hours pushing out a lizard. It's not polite—or safe.

When I posted the first photos of my precious daughter, I was flooded with positive comments and emails saying how beautiful she was; the words "stunning" and "gorgeous" were used frequently. Then I would see the same people post the *exact same* comments on other newborn photos. It wasn't their lack of creativity I had a problem with; it was the fact that these other newborns were so, so far from stunning or gorgeous. What were the chances that my kid was the only one they were telling the truth about? I thought back to the unibrow situation in my own newborn photo, and I realized that the gorgeous odds weren't exactly in Vivian's favor.

Most of my MOFLs agree that your newborn is not cute, and they will admit that their babies weren't Gerber quality either at first.

Jill, mom of twins, says, "Hey, mine were furry and had floppy ears like puppies when they were born."

Michelle agrees. "All newborns are ugly. All of them."

Dana has a very scientific explanation for the denial: "I honestly think it's a hormone that puts beer goggles on you for the first few weeks. Looking back at pictures, you'll realize they are never as cute as you remember."

The funniest part of this chapter is the fact that even though you've read and absorbed it, you still won't believe it to be true when your little one arrives. You'll turn to family and friends in the hospital and ask for reassurance: "Seriously, she's beautiful, right? It's not just me?" And they will all nod and fawn over the baby. Why? Because they have the love goggles on, too. Or they don't have the heart to tell you that you have given birth to an alien.

9

IT MAY NOT BE LOVE AT FIRST SIGHT

(mostly because at first sight
the child looks like an alien)

The people you will actually love at first sight:

- The Epidural Man

- The Magical Nurse who can soothe your baby with the perfect swaddle

- The first friend or family member who brings you a hamburger and fries in the hospital

- Whoever introduces you to stool softeners

A proven fact:
You will love your baby 162 times more when they are sleeping.

A piece of advice:
Take lots of pictures of your baby when they are sleeping; flip through them when they are screaming.

Before I experienced childbirth I expected it to be a lot like I had seen in the movies. Where a woman with perfect makeup (and no pregnancy weight on her face) scoops up her newborn as soon as it pops out, looks deep into its little eyes, and instantly falls head over heels in love. I was expecting appropriately inspiring music to begin playing in the background. It would be all peace and love and soft lighting.

Fast-forward to my own childbirth experience in which I was wheeled into the hospital screaming my face off and then handed a baby about an hour later. But when I held the baby, that overwhelming feeling of love and peace didn't happen. And the lighting was terrible. I instantly had an overwhelming need to protect her, but my life didn't go from black and white to color the way I'd heard other mothers describe it. Instead, everything just stayed the same hue.

Initially I blamed my lack of instant affection on the insanity that preceded my baby's arrival. That rollercoaster (a unique rollercoaster that included only the free-fall portion) left me a bit spent immediately following the delivery. As soon as Vivian popped out, I just laid my head back on the bed, looked at my mom, and said, "That was insane." I tried to calm myself down from the insanity while my partner stayed with the baby, who was under a heat lamp like McDonald's French fries, getting toasty for her official introduction to the world.

After Vivian was done cooking, the nurse brought her over and instantly started shoving my boob into her mouth (in Vivian's mouth, not the nurse's—that would have been awkward) while roughly fourteen other hospital people milled about on computers, machines, and my crotch. It was less than serene, to say the least. But still, I was surprised that I didn't have the jolt of affection I was expecting.

Then a parade of friends and family started coming through the room, all wanting to snuggle the new baby. Before she arrived, I had expected that I wouldn't enjoy this part, allowing anyone else to hold my newborn when I really wanted to keep her all to myself. But when the time came I was happy to pass her around. People were excited to meet her and take pictures, and I was an emotionless, horrible mother, so it all worked out.

Even when we got settled into our own room, with just us and the baby, I was still waiting for the love to kick in. I watched over her every second, asked thirteen million questions about how to best care for her, and held her close as much as possible, but all that felt mechanical in a sense. The only real emotion I had was when I watched her sleeping in that little plastic bassinet next to me. It broke my heart that she looked so alone and cold, after having been warm and protected inside of me for so many months. But when I would hold her and whisper "I love you" into her little ear 3,764 times a day, I still felt as if I was trying to convince both of us.

By the time I got home I felt like pretty much the worst mom in the history of the planet because my emotions had not registered the appropriate level of love for my child. I was going through all the motions of caring for her and doing all the things a loving mother should, but I still didn't feel a connection to her. I couldn't believe that all the time I'd spent talking to her and praying for her while she was inside of me didn't translate to an instant bond once she was outside. All the color was changing in my world, but it was going in the wrong direction.

Looking back on this time now, I see that I was struggling for a multitude of reasons, the most significant being the postpartum depression I was experiencing. The inadequacy I felt because I didn't instantly bond with my baby just added to my long list of things to feel bad about. Also, I didn't really feel comfortable talking about this lack of emotion with anyone, for fear that they would confirm my belief that I was a horrible mother. It was all very isolating.

A few weeks after Vivian arrived, I leaned down and whispered into her ear, "I love you," like I had countless times before. But this time, suddenly, I actually felt it. I wanted to shake her and say, "No really! I mean it this time! This is huge!" Vivian just snuggled up against my boob and closed her eyes, as if to say, "Yeah, welcome to the party. The rest of us have been here for a while."

I think the biggest hurdle for me, beyond my emotional state, was the fact that I had essentially given birth to a blob. For the first little while, there was a lot of tending to her every need but with little coming back from her (unless you count the spit-up). It sounds horrible, but when you are trying to connect with someone and they aren't really involved in the relationship, it can be rather difficult. But slowly she started to wake up: Her little eyes opened and started actually taking in her surroundings. She would give the occasional smile (usually this was the result of gas, but I took it), and her arms and legs began moving all over the place, as if she were officially ready for this race to begin. She was becoming a little person, and the more I got to know that person, the more I fell in love with her.

I share my story with you because this issue is one that is pretty common but not really discussed much. It has come up in my conversation with moms, but it's always spoken of long after the time when they were doubting their emotions toward their child. When they were actually going through their struggles, they felt very alone, especially when surrounded by ridiculously happy people who would say things like, "A new baby! You must be over the moon with excitement!"

Which leaves moms wondering, *Why am I not over the f'n moon? What is wrong with me?*

My answer to that is: Nothing. Nothing is wrong with you. Your body is a hormonal mess, you aren't sleeping, and you are completely overwhelmed. You just need a second to get up to speed on the bonding-with-your-child thing. Do yourself a favor and give yourself some time to settle in before you start entering Worst Mother of the Year contests. Go through the motions, hold your baby close to you, tell them you love them more than anything in the world. And eventually you will, I promise.

I reached out to my MOFLs to see if they, too, had struggled with bonding initially. Unfortunately I started with Chipper Jen.

"I fell in LOVE with my babies in the womb!!! I wanted kids my whole life and had pretty much figured out that I'm on this earth to be a mom! The second they were laid on my chest I cried with emotion because I never wanted to let them go! I never knew what love was until I held them in my arms!! Priceless!"

Great.

Then Kaysee, mom of three, piled it on even more. "I really felt so in love with my babies when they were born. But, my births were not very traumatic at all. I have always bonded with them right away!"

Two for two. Maybe I am the worst mom in the world.

Thankfully, Sarah came to my rescue. "Dawn, I'm with you. I liked Drew a LOT! But the absolute love came a little later. I just needed to get to know him. But with Owen it was right away, I think because I knew what to expect. Things are much different the second time. With Drew I literally had no idea what to expect about anything, and I was afraid of the birth and afraid of him! So I think that had a lot to do with it."

Thank God! There is another mom in the world who understands me.

The other Sarah had different experiences with her different births. "With my first, we bonded immediately. My pregnancy and delivery with him were high risk and traumatic, so I felt a kinship with him immediately. Like we were little warriors together!"

However, her second delivery was not quite the same. "I took a few weeks to bond with my second baby. I think there were multiple things going on. I had waves of guilt and sadness during pregnancy, like I was taking something away from my first child. I worried how the second baby's presence would affect my relationship with my first baby. I also had really hoped Theo was a girl, and during labor my doctor and nurse thought they felt a vagina (he was breech), so it was discombobulating when a giant boy came out. The last and main reason I think I had trouble bonding with him was that he was delivered via C-section. I truly believe, for me, it was easier to bond with Jake and Bea because they were born as I expected, with no major surprises. And like you said, I had immense affection and protection of him immediately, but I felt more like a babysitter than his mom. It was so sad and I was so sad!"

One of my MOFLs, Jenine, has a rather unique take on this issue, and I found it to be amazing. Here is her story in full:

"I gave a baby up for adoption when I was seventeen years old. A bunch of well-meaning women told me repeatedly how hard the birth was going to be on me. How I was going to fall so in love with this baby there was no way anyone was going to take her from me. But when the time came I handed her off without even one tear. She was beautiful and I was very happy that she was healthy, but that's about it.

"So for the next fourteen years I was worried that I was a heartless bitch. What kind of woman doesn't love her daughter? I worried endlessly about not loving a baby when my time came to have one and raise it.

"When my son was born and had to go right to the NICU for a few days, I was beside myself that I needed to be holding him and bonding with him. (I had read that the first six days were the most important bonding time and had a very specific plan to make sure it happened.) I was convinced that I would never love him as a mother should. It was terrible. My husband had no idea what to do with me. The bonding came with him after a few days or weeks, and in hindsight I wish I had told someone how worried I was about the whole thing, so they could have helped me calm my fears.

"Turns out I loved my first baby a bunch, too, and I was very happy that she was going to be in a perfect, beautiful home with two parents who loved her just as much as I did. I could have saved myself a lot of grief if I'd figured this out earlier! My first daughter is now almost eighteen years old, and I have kept in touch with her and her family throughout her life. The two of us are training for a half-marathon together now. On a long run recently I told her this story, and she stopped running for a second and with glassy eyes said, 'Giving me my family was the most love you could possibly have shown me!' Seriously! She's pretty amazing!"

How great is that story? I love happy endings!!

If you are having trouble bonding with your baby, even if you can't bring yourself to talk to someone about how you are feeling, read over these stories again and know that you are not a bad mother, or even all that different from a lot of mothers out there (except for Chipper Jen, but she is on a totally different level than the rest of us). Just as they have for all of us who have struggled, things will fall into place for you, and eventually you'll get that feeling you were expecting from the very beginning. And it will only get better and better as time goes by (because as time goes by they begin to sleep more . . .).

PARTNER CORNER: BONDING WITH BABY

Pat: Skin to skin is very important. I think being present is important as well. But for the first three months, the baby just sleeps, eats, and shits, so don't expect to have a bond with the baby right away. That comes after three, six, nine months. I also was the one giving baths a lot, so that helped with being present at times.

Larry: I constantly made myself available to my wife and new child. I was NEVER too tired for a feeding, especially if my wife needed a break and it wasn't "my turn." If I was sitting watching sports or a movie, I was skin to skin with my new baby. Possibly with a beer in hand.

Tom: For the times when the baby wasn't breastfeeding directly but drinking pre-pumped milk, I would try to do as many of those feedings as I could. It felt good to have one-on-one time, even if it was 3 a.m.

Jason: Look, I was basically talked into having a baby because my wife wanted one. I didn't have that emotional rush that she had, but I did immediately skin-to-skin hold him . . . for hours, on those first few days. I think somehow that helped. But now that my son is six, every moment of that time in the beginning led to our amazing relationship now. He's my "mini-me," and there's really nothing better than our time together. But for the first six months . . . he was an eating/pooping machine, and it took time for my relationship to really develop.

10

NO ONE IS LOVING THIS AS MUCH AS THEIR FACEBOOK POSTS WOULD HAVE YOU BELIEVE

(don't trust the comment section either)

The bad news:

Social media requires that you post regular photos of your adorable child.

The badder news:

Your child is probably not actually adorable.

The good news:

At least you are no longer required to post attractive pictures of yourself.

The gooder news:

Which is good, because there isn't a filter strong enough to smooth out what is happening on your face.

I find that there are two basic types of people who post on social media, those whose lives are "AWESOME, SO PERFECT, OH MY GOODNESS, LOOK HOW GREAT THIS SALAD IS THAT I'M EATING!" and those whose monologue goes, "Everything sucks. Life sucks. I lost my phone again. I don't have enough money to buy a taco. Sad face. Sigh." Apparently, from the extensive research I've conducted of my social media feeds, as soon as you have children you must, must, must fall into the first category, no questions asked. Every post must be about how much you love your baby and your life and should also include a photo of your child being adorable (please see Chapter 8, "Your Newborn Is Not Cute," for clarification on whether those photos are actually adorable).

Here's the problem with all this: I know for a fact that despite our postings to the contrary, not every parent thinks everything is so perfect and awesome *all* the time. So why do we all feel the need to lie to the internets?

Do you remember back before the constant exchange of life facts via the web, when people had to send yearly holiday letters describing the wonderful wonders that the family had experienced throughout the year? When I was a kid I used to love reading those letters, littered with children's accomplishments and parents' praise: "Jennifer is the school president!" "Phillip is the captain of the football team!" And there was always one kid you could sense was a hard sell every year: "Jimmy loves P.E. this year!" Each Christmas the same families would send their yearly updates, and I always wondered if every year the parents stressed over whether their kids were going to do anything noteworthy enough to boast about on pretty paper.

Now that the internet has taken the place of silly things such as writing on pretty paper, our lives have gone from once-a-year updates to multiple-times-a-day updates. This puts parents in a bit of a bind. All day they have to see other parents post about how wonderful their children are, how great their partner is—how even their dogs are exceptional. The pressure mounts as they read each post because they feel as if they need make positive posts about their brood as well. No longer do you have an entire year to gather noteworthy tidbits.

So between the baby screaming her face off for three hours straight and the toddler swinging the cat around by its tail, Mom is able to snap one nonblurry photo and post it to Facebook/Twitter/Instagram with the tagline "So blessed!" Then she promptly goes back to yelling at the dog to stop barking at every leaf that falls outside. This, in turn, sets off another mom who tries to prop her newborn up on the couch for an adorable photo that ends up looking like a picture of your drunk uncle after too much Christmas eggnog. "Love my life!!"

It's a weird thing, this unconscious competition among women and parents on social media, all trying to convince the world (themselves?) that everything is always going smashingly, when in fact we would all be drawn together a lot more if we posted more in the vein of "Seriously, at some point the baby HAS to sleep, right? I'm losing my mind over here."

It's an interesting thing to follow friends and family when they have a new baby. The first few days the social media posts are hot and heavy. Pictures galore, loving their new angel, so very blessed, everyone healthy and happy. Then you can sense the shift after they get home. Most post only sporadically, the occasional photo of their sleeping baby (sleeping babies are the cutest babies) or a positive comment about how great things are going. But there are always a few who stop posting altogether. Once-habitual Facebook updaters go eerily silent.

I'm sure there are a lot of reasons for this, the number one being they have a few other things besides social media to think about now. But for some I know there is something more going on. They are struggling, and they can't muster the super-excited posts they think are expected of them, or at least they are expecting of themselves. And heaven forbid they post what they are really feeling— overwhelmed and tired—because that wouldn't fit with all the positive posts they see from other parents. It's sad that parents shy away from social media during the times when it could really help. Kind words and supportive comments would be good for our exhausted spirit and could even bring welcome advice to help moms navigate.

It is really important to know that despite the constant positive Facebook posts, every parent everywhere has struggles throughout the day. No parent has ever gotten to bedtime and thought, *Man, that was my A+ game. I did every single thing right and nothing went wrong. I should host a show on how to do this!* We are all out there doing the best we can, and more likely than not we post our positive pictures and comments to keep our own spirits up, not to bring anyone else's down.

As you venture onto this new parenting terrain, don't hesitate to call on help and advice from your social media friends. I have constantly posted questions and complaints (Me complaining? Shocking, I know.) on my social media since my daughter arrived. I am always quite touched by the responses I get, some helpful, others comforting, and some downright hilarious. It's a nice little community of moms who, despite their upbeat posts, have struggled as well and are happy to share what they've learned along the way.

If you don't feel comfortable posting your questions or issues to the masses, you can also find moms-only groups on social media, or you can create a separate Facebook list for friends you trust and whose opinions you value—then post your more personal thoughts for only that group to see. Although do consider opening that list up to more than just your closest friends. Some of the best advice I've received has been from people I haven't seen in years, who apparently have been quite busy making and raising babies, while also accumulating hard-won parenting lessons. In fact, add anyone to the list who has two or more children. They are encyclopedias of knowledge, just waiting to explode wisdom all over you.

11

YOU JUST POOPED OUT A BABY (YOUR BODY POST-BABY)

(unfortunately that visual is not nearly as traumatizing as what actually happened)

After my lovely, wonderful little baby arrived, I held her in my arms in the hospital and said, "I can't believe I just pooped her out!"

My mom looked at me sideways and said, "That's not *exactly* what happened."

To which I replied, "Well, that's *exactly* what it felt like."

And if you have a vaginal birth, that is exactly what it will feel like for quite some time. I've been told, and have even read online, that childbirth is the most natural process in the world, but the amount of tearing of private areas that occurs during that process leads me to believe there has got to be one or two things that are a little more natural. And when you can't even poop right for weeks after your natural childbirth, you start to think maybe nature has taken a turn for the worse.

Before I had my baby, I was planning on a birth drenched in epidurals ("Give me all the drugs!!"). I was very surprised to find out that not only was I able to push the watermelon out of my whooha drug-free, but that I was expected to get upright and go for a stroll mere minutes after the delivery.

When I sat up in the bed I felt a gush come out of me that I was not looking forward to sharing with the floor. "Um, there is going to be a lot of stuff... I can feel it . . ." The nurse just nodded her head and told me it was fine. I understand that they see gushes of blood come from private areas every day, but it still seemed rather alarming when it came pouring out of my areas as I stood up. Drip, drip, drip—I made it to the bathroom where the same nurse had me sit on the toilet while she used various squirt bottles to clean me off. And here I thought having people in close proximity to my nether regions was done for the day. But no.

And this time I didn't have the excitement and chaos of a child-birth to distract me from the fact that a stranger was concentrating very hard on my very private areas. Squirt, squirt, squirt. I just looked all around the bathroom, trying to avoid any direct eye contact, wondering if this is what this woman had dreamt of when she decided to go into the medical field. I'm thinking this particular job requirement isn't highlighted in the brochures.

Even after that spray down the blood kept coming, and it didn't stop coming for weeks. My body apparently had a lot of purging to do following its forty-week creation of a person. I wondered if it would ever stop, or if my body was perhaps having a huge period to compensate for the several it had missed over the months. This is the "crime scene" time, as referred to by Chipper Jen, so that gives you a good idea of what you are in for.

I had a natural childbirth with no real complications, besides an episiotomy (if you don't know what that is, DO NOT look it up), and yet I still had some uncomfortable physical issues following the birth. I imagine there is no way to get a watermelon out of your uterus without some lingering physical issues, so I'm not sure why I was so taken aback by the ones I experienced.

My biggest recommendation for a more comfortable post-baby experience: stool softeners, lots of them. Stools can never really be too soft, it turns out. And you don't really want to find out what it feels like when they aren't soft enough, trust me. In general, all things bathroom related are off limits in our household conversation, but post-baby those rules went out the window. My poor partner was sent to the store for the most unfortunate combination of products having to do with stools, hemorrhoids, and numbing. There's a possibility that checking out with all that stuff was even more painful than being the one who needed it.

Also, even if you don't feel like you need them in the hospital, go ahead and take those extra-strength Motrin they offer you before you leave. I had terrible cramping after I got home, and Motrin was the only thing that could alleviate the pain. They also offered me Vicodin, but that seemed a bit excessive and unnecessary, especially considering I was breastfeeding. They said it was fine to take while breastfeeding, but it didn't seem right to me, so I stuck to the occasional Motrin.

And speaking of breastfeeding. My boobs were Out. Of. Control. You would think I was feeding a small army of children given how big my girls got. I could tell that their size increased quite a bit because when I saw friends, their eyes would instantly go to my boobs. Instantly. And most of the time they wouldn't even do the standard quick recovery back up to my eyes; they would linger on the boobs for quite a while. On more than one occasion I was asked if I had gotten a boob job, because that seemed like a totally normal thing for a new mom to do, apparently.

Although my ginormous boobs were a sight to behold, they were sensitive beyond belief, which made even simple tasks a bit of a hassle. I had been so excited to sleep on my stomach again post-baby, after months of side sleeping, but with my two painful traffic-cone boobs, it was a while before sleeping on my belly was a comfortable option again. I would try to play catch with the dogs outside, but anything faster than a slow walk had the girls bobbin' and hurtin'. And oh my goodness, why do people *insist* on hugging so much??? Can we stick with only elbow bumps please?

I wanted to get you some details on other post-baby issues and was worried that my MOFLs would be hesitant to share such private information. Who really wants to talk about all this uncomfortable stuff? It's not exactly dinner party chatter.

That is, unless you get a bunch of moms together and start asking them what happened to their bodies after they had their babies. Then it's on. And it's hilarious. In a very painful, I-need-to-ice-my-whooha-after-just-hearing-these-stories sort of way.

Consider yourself warned.

Jill, mom of twins, was lucky enough to have one of her babies via vaginal delivery and one via Cesarean, because who doesn't want to experience it all? "I had a vaginal delivery and a C-section and a tear in my cervix that all had to be 'fixed' before I went to recovery. I also couldn't hold the kids at all since they were so tiny. It was awful. Then I couldn't even drive for a few weeks and had to get rides to the hospital."

The lack of driving and general mobility seems to be the biggest pain with Cesareans. Sarah, mom of three, had an unplanned Cesarean with her second child. "The Frankenstein staples were gross. The nurses were FANTASTIC because I'd had a C-section. I couldn't go upstairs for a week or drive for two, but otherwise not a big deal. Much, much easier recovery than my first delivery. Except I couldn't poop for days and also became addicted to stool softeners!"

Sarah also didn't have as easy a time with her natural birth. "After my first birth I looked like a stoned fat lady who had just gotten in a gang fight. Two black eyes, all the whites of my eyes were red, my face was swollen so much I literally could not open my eyes.

Then the bitchy nurses refused to help me to the bathroom since I wasn't a C-section. Only problem, I collapsed spontaneously due to nerve damage from an injection to stop bleeding. I LOVED when they woke me up in the middle of the night to aggressively massage my fundus. Several weeks after delivery, I delivered a clot the size of a baby's head." But there was one bright spot. "Both times my boobs were huge and rock hard. I remember looking at myself and thinking I looked sexy. I had gigantic boobs and my stomach had gone down."

Chipper Jen had some unfortunate leaking. "Mine wasn't bad except the contractions after the second child were HORREN-DOUS!! Labor was easier than that! And I had awful bladder issues! Leaked all the time. Bent over, leak. Walked down the stairs—leak, leak, leak. Like a ninety-year-old."

Erika had an experience that was a little more traumatizing. "I swear my first post-baby bowel movement was worse than the birthing experience . . . also, hemorrhoids, hemorrhoids, hemorrhoids."

And, to finish us off, I have the best story that has ever been told in the history of women telling horrendous stories about their bodies post-childbirth, and it comes from Amy: "My worst experience was with my first pregnancy. She was large (eight pounds, thirteen ounces), with a beautifully round head. I had a third-degree tear, even with an episiotomy. I felt like I was healing okay and assumed the pain I was feeling was the tear healing plus hemorrhoids. It wasn't until my six-week checkup that my doctor asked how I was functioning with the tear in my rectum. I had no idea! I was sent to a colorectal specialist, and, after trying several types of medicine (including a nitroglycerin compound that had to be made at a special pharmacy), I ended up having surgery four months after she was born to repair the tear. He even injected me with Botox in that area to relax the muscles and speed healing."

And here Amy provides the single best line of my entire book, so cherish it, dear readers: "The result? I now have the asshole of a twenty-year-old but have to take fiber the rest of my life like a seventy-year-old."

And there you have it. Is there anything more beautiful than creating life? If you are lucky you will get a new baby AND a new butthole!

12

YOUR LIFE IS OFFICIALLY OVER

(it had a good run)

Before baby	vs.	After baby
"Why do stores close so early? It's only midnight!!"		"Why do stores open so late? I've been up since 4:00 a.m.!!"

Everything will now take 562,035 times as long to do (e.g., getting ready in the morning, going to bed at night, getting out of the house).

Except the things you will have to learn to do 562,035 times as fast (e.g., changing a poopy diaper, covering yourself up and whipping your boob out, packing up and getting out of any location when your child starts to have an epic meltdown).

have some bad news. That life you've grown accustomed to? It's long, far away, never to be seen again gone. May it rest in peace. (Which is ironic, because you will not be resting in peace, or any other state, for quite some time.)

All the things that you've taken for granted will be things of the past. Sleep, freedom, spare time, and . . . well, those are the big three that cover pretty much all the good things in life. Fortunately, those wonderful things will be replaced by baby giggles and smiles (and baby farts, which for some reason are endlessly entertaining), so at least some bright spots remain on your horizon.

My biggest new baby adjustment, by far, was the change in my sleep schedule. At first this change meant going from sleeping as long as I wanted, at whatever time I wanted, to not sleeping more than two hours at a time. Even now, with the baby sleeping through the night, I haven't quite gotten used to going to bed early and getting up early, because it's just not what my body has been doing for the past decade or so. And it's not going down without a fight.

When you add the change in sleep schedule to the general energy drain of awake children, you end up with a constant feeling of exhaustion. A feeling that I imagine will be present for the next couple of decades. You might want to invest in some of that miracle cream that eliminates dark circles under your eyes. Or just start saving for some major plastic surgery: *a hundred dollars for the kid's college fund, a hundred dollars for Mommy's face reconstruction fund*. I'm sure it will be tax deductible, as soon as there is a woman president.

The loss of freedom will also take you by surprise, even if you thought you were prepared for it. For a few years before I had a child, I made a very big effort to maximize my freedom, knowing that it was going to take a hit when a baby came along. I traveled all over the place, ate out at restaurants several times a week, and basically did whatever I wanted, whenever I wanted—even if most of the time all I really wanted to do was watch an entire TV season on Netflix in one day. I was crazy adventurous like that. But on the whole, I was in that rare sweet spot where I had the finances and freedom to support whatever I was interested in doing with my time. And I had a countdown clock pushing me to have as much fun and relaxation as possible before it ran out.

Then it ran out.

Even though I had spent years "preparing" for my loss of freedom, it turns out all I was really doing was setting myself up for the loss to be an even bigger hit to my lifestyle. Things went upside down overnight. I remember standing outside a baby store one morning with a group of other moms, all of us holding our children and waiting for the store to open. I had already been awake for so many hours, and yet this store still wasn't open. How was this possible? When in the history of me had I ever had the occasion to be anywhere early enough to be the first one there? And how sad were all of us moms standing outside tapping on the window, begging them to open so we could buy our diapers and cheap toys?

Things were equally altered during the nighttime hours. I remember when we were thinking of moving to the suburbs, for a bigger house and a safer neighborhood, and a (childless) friend of mine just shook her head. "You know, it's nice out there, but there is absolutely no nightlife."

That was by far the funniest thing I had heard in all my days: the thought that (1) I would be making any choice about anything based on nightlife and (2) I still had a nightlife that didn't include a night light.

Gone were the days of spontaneously going out for dinner and a movie, maybe catching some theater in the city on a whim. Instead of saying, "Hey, what do you want to do tonight?" we would now say, "Hey, I hope the baby sleeps more than four hours in a row tonight."

Our social calendar basically just included major holidays, when we were forced by society to put the child in a festive outfit and leave the house. Other than that, our biggest plans involved the nonstop fun of tummy time and the occasional head cold.

One night Becky decided she wanted to expand our horizons and invite some people over for dinner. "Let's have them over on Friday! It'll be great. We'll cook and eat and—"

"They will not be available on Friday."

"Why?"

"Because it's Wednesday today and they don't have children. They have lives. Lives that have been planned for a couple weeks."

She began to send them a text message, perhaps suffering from amnesia about what her life used to be like. "They will be able to— oh, never mind, they wrote back. They aren't free this Friday or any Friday for the next month."

Somehow, in the midst of all this not sleeping or having fun, your life will take yet another odd hit. Suddenly, for no comprehensible reason, your days will become entirely too short to get anything done at all. Where you used to be able to kick the crap out of a to-do list, you now won't even be able to find the list, let alone kick any part of it. This will be absolutely baffling from a mathematical standpoint. If anything, your days have gotten longer, with that whole lack of sleep thing. But somehow your productivity has come to a standstill.

You used to handle your to-do list and unwind by watching a little TV or reading magazines and even tackling *entire* novels. Sometimes really long novels. Now you are lucky to catch a glimpse of Facebook while breastfeeding the baby before you both pass out. "Downtime" has taken on a new meaning, too, in that it is time you spend literally "down" on the floor playing with the baby (or at least pretending to play with the baby while you actually try to catch a quick catnap while lying on the floor with the kid).

Before Vivian came along, I was crazy productive. I had a career and hobbies and attended social events. And I slept twelve hours a night. In my remaining twelve hours a day, I could jam out all sorts of projects, lunch dates, soccer games, writing sessions, and even the occasional day spent movie-hopping at the theater. And I *still* slept twelve hours a day. That's some time-management prowess right there.

These days, I can't even remember the last time I went to a movie, I'm too tired to play soccer, and going on a lunch date messes up an entire day of work. At the end of most days, I feel like I've added more things to my to-do list than I've subtracted. My kid is a year and a half, and in those eighteen months I've yet to have a day where I've said to myself, "All caught up!!" There's always more stuff to be done and never quite enough time.

But as my daughter gets older, images of my old life fade away, and this new life comes more and more into focus. My days haven't gotten shorter, per se; they have just been filled with a new little person. When she was brand new, I would literally spend hours just staring at my new little person. (Which was about half wonder and half thousand-yard stare.) Now, instead of watching TV and reading novels, I spend my time singing the alphabet and playing with stickers. (So. Many. Stickers.) At least once a day, and usually more, my kid will do something that nearly makes my heart explode because it reminds me how much I love her. She gives standing ovations for the most mundane accomplishments and gently puts her head against the cat to give it hugs. She passes out kisses with abandon. She's not a bad way to spend a day, is what I'm saying.

In the beginning, when your old life is still only a few weeks or months in the rearview mirror, everything can seem so overwhelmingly different. It's not that your new schedule is bad, it's just SO DIFFERENT. You might need a minute to adjust to that life U-turn. The fact that it takes a minute doesn't make you ungrateful or a bad parent. It just makes you a human who is tasked with navigating a new, poop-filled route.

I can't tell you that it gets so much easier and you'll be back enjoying the nightlife again in no time, because that is probably not going to happen. But I can tell you that your new nightlife, with bath time and story time and bedtime, will eventually feel pretty nice, too (mostly because it ends with the child sleeping).

Even though you are probably exhausted at the end of your new daily routine, try to force yourself to unwind once your little one is down, even if it's just for a half hour or so. Turn on the TV, take six months to read that new novel, talk to your spouse about something other than your child's bowel movements. You know, get back to the glamorous parts of life. Maybe even put on a strobe light and rip up twenty-dollar bills, so you can still get a taste of that old nightlife.

I asked my MOFLs what they miss most about their lives pre-baby and the things they love most about their new lives. So much sweetness ensued.

Sarah says, "I miss SLEEP!!!!!! Also, my freedom and time alone. I love rocking Drew to sleep every night and all the crazy, funny stuff he says. And Owen's first smiles and giggles."

Michelle is not a fan of the mess. "I miss my house actually staying clean for more than five minutes after I clean it. The thing I love the most is when Enzo says 'I wuv you Mommy!' without me saying it first."

Jenine could go for a little quiet. "I love and hate all the talking from my four-year-old. He is hilarious!! But then, he also never shuts up. I almost never listen to music or watch TV when he's not around anymore because I am relishing the silence!! My two kids just started playing together a little, and I cannot get enough of it! They crack each other up, and it makes me feel all warm and smooshy inside. Yeah, freedom would be nice. Like the freedom to use the bathroom or take a shower without planning it out."

Dana says, "I miss the normal stuff: going to dinner with my husband on a random weeknight because we can, being able to leave the house without thinking about diapers, a change of clothes, burp cloths, toys, etc. I miss being alone and going to the gym. The things I love are just watching my kids grow. Prior to having kids I never really had a reason to pay attention to how amazing early child development is. I am literally surprised every day by something new that comes out of Reese's mouth or some new milestone my baby just hit. It's just really fun and really amazing at the same time. Oh, and when Reese will tell me she loves me out of nowhere. That is pretty much the best thing on earth!"

Carrie misses the gym, but it's more than just the sweating she longs for. "I, too, miss the gym, or what it represents. Time alone, time without a stopwatch ticking. Especially after the second baby, it's ten times harder. However, I love their laughs and smiles. Now with the talking and questions, it's so fun to see their little minds working. Also, I love the early-morning cuddles. I wouldn't miss those for the world!"

So you see, even though your life is in fact over, it is being re-placed with something new. New adventures, new fun, and new ways to deal with sleep deprivation. Somewhere on the horizon, just past diaper rashes and sleepless nights, lies a moment when the love of your life will walk up for no reason and say, "I love you, Mama." Then, all of a sudden, sleep and freedom will seem very, very small in comparison. If you're lucky, they'll even throw in a baby fart to keep the mood light.

PARTNER CORNER: YOUR NEW LIFE

Pat: First off . . . you never get to sleep on your own schedule ever again. No sleeping in, no staying up late. . . . You now have turned into your grandparents, and 9:15 p.m. is the new 1 a.m. Also, no more "quick" weekend trips. You now will overpack for everything, and you will use none of it. Be prepared.

Tom: The one difference that stuck with me was the disconnect with pop culture. Before kids, I would be talking with friends who had newborns and ask, "Did you see this movie (or TV show)?" and the answer would usually be no. C'mon, what are they DOING with all their time? Ah, I see now . . .

Larry: The biggest change for us was the of loss of free time. A common question . . . in our home was, "What did we do with our time before kids?" In the beginning, the children became our new and only hobby. It wasn't until the toddler phase of our first child that we learned to balance what we needed to do and what we wanted to do as adults.

Jason: I still miss going out to dinner every night. Sex when we wanted it. Going to a foreign country because there was a cheap deal next week. That life is DEAD. Plain and simple. And part of me does miss that life, I won't lie. But . . . if you asked me to give back my kid in exchange for that life, there's no way in hell I'd ever consider it. Yeah, it's different. But it's like a higher level of fulfillment.

Some philosopher talked about the higher level of pleasure, like would you rather be a pig rolling around in the mud or at the opera? Of course, the pig in mud is happy—that was me before kids—and now there's way more obligations, my time is more limited, my freedoms are limited . . . but I have the higher-level joys that I never would've experienced.

13

POOP, PUKE, AND PEE

(the trifecta will getcha)

POOP CLEANING REQUIREMENTS

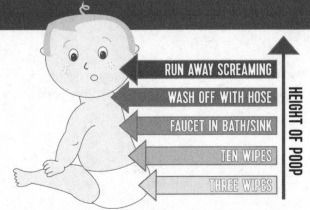

RUN AWAY SCREAMING

WASH OFF WITH HOSE

FAUCET IN BATH/SINK

TEN WIPES

THREE WIPES

HEIGHT OF POOP

Times you mention poop per day pre-baby	vs.	Times you mention poop per day post-baby
0 (or 2 if you have animals)		2,965,283 (or 3,541,146 if your child is not pooping or pooping too much)

Your least favorite word pre-baby	vs.	Your least favorite word post-baby
Monday		Projectile

An actual conversation:

"Hey! There is poop in her belly button! How did you miss that?!"

"I'm sorry, I didn't think to look for poop in her belly button! Sorta the opposite location of where I was looking."

L et's just cut right to the chase: Things are going to get messy. And not as in "Oh, you dripped a little ketchup on your shirt while eating a burger." Oh no. More of a "Seriously, how long has that poop been on my shirt with no one pointing it out??" Where once your life was pristine and tasteful, it is now covered in things that came out of different parts of a human being.

It is absolutely unreal how much stuff comes out of a thing that weighs less than ten pounds. And yet, it becomes very real, very fast. This brings us to the number-one rule for successfully parenting a newborn. Number one. Are you listening?

Always, always, ALWAYS put a new diaper under the baby before you take off the old diaper. Say it with me now. Remember it forever. And always, always, ALWAYS have a diaper on the child (bathe them in a diaper to be really safe). The ONE time you forget to put a diaper under the baby or decide to hold the baby without a diaper on, you will go from "Oh my goodness look how cute that little bottom is!" to "Oh, oh no, she's . . . shit! It's on my arm, on the floor! There's shit everywhere!!" I promise you that this progression of events and emotions can all occur within a span of time that seems almost scientifically impossible.

In fact, go ahead and get used to the phrase, "There's shit everywhere!" It will become a frequent battle cry in the first few months. (The shit doesn't stop after the first few months; you just build up a tolerance that makes you unshockable in regard to feces. Parenting is a joy and a miracle. A joy and a miracle.)

Vivian had what we liked to refer to as a "Poop Show," and man, was it an event to behold. On not-so-rare occasions, Vivi would present to us her most awe-inspiring skill: the poop/pee combination. She was super-proud of this skill and wanted to make sure we got a chance to see it for ourselves, so she would wait until her diaper was off to perform. Most of the time she would wait until her old diaper was off, but riiiiight before the new one was in place—she was that talented and precise in her execution.

The encore to the Poop Show in the beginning (before we followed the number-one rule) went like this: "Oh crap, it's everywhere. I have to pull the cover off the changing table before trying to put on a new diaper—because it's everywhere and there's no safe place to put her." Pick up the child. Then, when pulling the changing table cover off, Vivian would either (1) continue the Poop Show on my arm or (2) puke all over my shoulder, completing her trifecta assault. And scene. Cue the applause.

I think the most startling thing about the abundance of poop is its ability to spread so quickly. I would constantly say, "The baby exploded." And if you were to look at the baby, you would have to agree that to be the only reasonable explanation for what you were witnessing. The line between cleaning a simple dirty diaper and having to rinse the child off using a power hose is very, very thin and can be hurdled over in a matter of seconds. And once the poop jumps the diaper barrier, everything in its path is destroyed. It's better to just look for a new place to live at that point.

My child had one particular pooping preference—or perhaps it was just her way of passing the time. Either way, just about every time I put her in her car seat, I would get to our destination to find a wonderful treasure waiting for me. Often that treasure was quite large, and because of the angle of her body in the seat, the diaper proved all but pointless. This habit of hers made our car rides oh so fun. I could see (her *very* serious face) and smell (a *very* serious smell) what was happening back there, and I could do nothing about it until I stopped driving. I would just silently wager myself on exactly how far up her back the poo would be when I took her out of her car seat / bathroom.

One time on the way to a playdate, when I had OF COURSE forgotten her diaper bag, Vivian OF COURSE exploded all over herself and her car seat. I had no choice but to enter the play place carrying my crap-covered child, praying that one of my friends had diapers and a change of clothes. As I was cleaning her on the floor, some of the other kids gathered around to observe the carnage. Weeks later one of the two-year-olds said to her mom, "Vivi stinky poo all over!" Exactly, Taylor, you just summed up life with a baby.

It seems all my MOFLs have a poop story to share—all of which paint quite a visual. One story even includes actual painting. Oh yes, we are keeping it classy.

Michelle tells of her son's skills: "I had the diaper almost off as Enzo projectile-pooped! It was the funniest thing ever." Some might not think the combination of the words "projectile" and "poop" would result in "funniest," but then you'd be forgetting the key ingredient: sleep deprivation—which makes everything really, really funny—or really, really sad. Michelle's advice for avoiding her hilarity: "Always use a changing pad of some sort, whether it be a blanket or a disposable pad, and always put the new diaper underneath the old one so you will be prepared for the unexpected!"

Karen has a lovely tale for you. "I put her down for a nap with no pants, just a shirt and diaper. The little wench pulled her diaper off and pooped all over the crib. Rolled around in it. Never woke up. It was in her hair and everywhere else. Moral of the story: always put pants on them once they are old enough to pull off their diapers."

To reinforce this point, Jenine pipes up, "My son had to wear footie pajamas, with the feet cut off, backwards so he couldn't get out of them. And for nap, a onesie OVER shorts or pants. It was the only way I could keep him from undressing. At first I said, 'Whatever, I'll clean up a little mess.' But then he finger painted with poo all over the place!!" This sounds like a scene from some sort of horror movie set in an insane asylum (a.k.a. living with a baby).

Here are the diaper tips we have for you during your stay in the asylum. They are simple but important.

1. Make sure there is something under your child when you are changing the diaper, something that can be discarded, cleaned, or burned if need be.
2. Invest in covers for the changing-pad covers: disposable little sheets of paper that go on top of the changing-table pad. Baby explodes, disposable sheet is disposed of. This will keep you from having to change and wash the fabric cover fifteen times a day.
3. In addition, make sure you put the new diaper under the baby's butt before you start dismantling the old diaper.
4. If this is all too much, just go to the sink or tub and fully bathe the kid before starting over.
5. Use the dirty diaper to get as much of the dirty business off as you can. Push down and wipe the kid's front, then pull up and wipe the kid's back—this cuts down on the 308 baby wipes you will need.
6. Have 308 baby wipes handy, always.
7. Travel with large Ziploc bags, and put dirty diapers in one, dirty clothes in another, protecting yourself and others from

the stench. Remove them when you get home and burn them all.

8. Note that diaper rash cream does not spread like lotion; you cannot just rub your hands together and absorb the excess into your pores. Remember this before you squirt way too much on your hands and end up getting it on every single part of the baby, not just his or her bottom.

9. Never leave the house without back-up clothes and maybe even a back-up to the back-ups. Babies tend to explode once they are outside the confines of their home. The farther they get from their house, the more likely it is that unfortunate things will start coming out of them. It's just science.

14

CHILDREN'S BOOKS ARE RIDICULOUS

(the only books that actually decrease your IQ)

Things I've learned from children's books:

- All animals, whether they be dogs, alligators, cows, or horses, can walk upright on their hind legs.

- Ten is as high as numbers go.

- There are a lot of purple animals in the world.

- Dora rhymes with "explorer."

- Wild animals really love being domesticated, especially the clothes-wearing part.

- All children are going to grow up to be firemen, teachers, princesses, or explorers—the next generation will be very short on cubicle workers who despise their jobs.

Things that are fun in children's books (and not so much in real life):

- Rodents

- Talking about bodily functions

- Believing that saying "please" and "thank you" will make anything possible

- Petting a crocodile

Books are a way for children to expand their brains and learn and grow and become literate geniuses, so why do I feel like I'm getting less intelligent every time I read one?

Books for kids fall into three categories: (Usually) Horrible Pictures / No Story, (Usually) Horrible Pictures / Nonsensical Story, and Let Me Try to Piss Off Hardworking Parents Everywhere by Selling a Million Copies of This Book That Took Me Four Minutes to Write.

My daughter's first books were some of the most ridiculous. They were those crinkly, puffy books for babies. They are officially called "Teethe and Read" books, and that name gives you a good idea of how much "reading" is actually intended. They have a handle on them (why don't all books have handles, now that I think about it), the corners have chewable plastic (because at that age everything is a teething toy), and they are a whopping six (crinkly) pages total. And wow do they weave a (totally incomprehensible) tale in those six pages.

Now, I understand that babies can't understand actual plotlines and aren't really concerned with such things, but couldn't the bookmakers (the word "authors" seems like a bit of a stretch here) extend a tiny tip of the cap to the poor parents who are going to be inevitably "reading" these books to the kids? Maybe at least try to include drawings that somehow form a story as the pages are turned? Based on my extensive independent studies of Vivian's pile of books, the answer to that question is a resounding no. They just pick six random drawings, throw them in the book, and ship them out to the confused teething masses. I guess when your target demo can't even control their own drool, character development is not a high priority.

For example, here is the story I would tell Vivian based on the drawings in one of her favorite (i.e., the one she ate the most) crinkle books:

A cow, an alligator, and a cat / possibly tiger are all hanging out. They are all the same size, which is super accurate to real life. The alligator is wearing a mitt and is ready to play baseball, but the cat thinks it might rain, which is why he has an umbrella. Turns out the cat was right! It's raining. Good thing the cat and his new buddy, the (very large) bug, have umbrellas. The alligator says, "Enough of this nonsense," and gets on a school bus with a horse, an elephant, maybe another horse, and that bug who was just holding the umbrella. It's not raining anymore, and again, because these animals are drawn completely to scale, they totally all fit on a bus together. Meanwhile, the cow is in a field stalking a pig in a dress. And the crocodile convinced the tiger to play baseball with him in another location. Then it's nighttime and the crocodile is hanging out in the field with a previously unseen lion. The end.

I will go ahead and spare you the ninety-minute monologue that ensued each time we "read" this book, in which I would go on and on about what a rip-off this book was and how it nearly costs as much as the book I wrote, which is two hundred pages and includes seventy thousand of my moderately thought-out words. Vivi would eventually try to shut me up by eating the book, hoping to devour it and thus eliminate any future tirades by her mother.

After the crinkly books, Viv moved on to the "Touch and Feel" books that have pictures of animals with fluffy material pasted to them. My favorite part of these books is that the "Touch and Feel" aspect of the book is not offered on *every* page, because that would be silliness. We pet a fluffy dog tail, then turn the page to find a duck with just a shiny piece of paper on its beak (rip-off), then a sheep with a little fluff, followed by a not-so-fluffy bucket or perhaps a tractor. Because who doesn't want to touch and feel metal? Oooh so snuggly.

Other favorites were the books that jump into the 3D/interactive realm with moving parts, flipping flaps revealing surprises, and other such excitement. These books seem like a ton of fun when purchased, and then you realize after fourteen seconds that your kid has ripped off every flipping flap and your book is essentially a naked shell, with all its surprises exposed. Nothing brings a children's book down quicker than flipping to a page and having to move a decapitated man back and forth along his little road to adventure (apparently this road was a rough one for him). These books are usually strewn around the house completely destroyed or covered in masking tape—with all the little heads and flaps and pop-up pieces reattached, Frankenstein-style.

My next effort to keep the child interested for more than three seconds were books that have the story and pictures on the left-hand side and buttons on the right-hand side that can be pushed to make fun sounds that go along with the reading. This was great! We would read the story, push the buttons at the correct time, and—"Honk! Honk!"—the baby would be enthralled in—"Chugga chugga chugga chugga chugga"—the excellent story and—"Honk! Honk!" What an audio adventure we would be taken on. But it turns out the only thing those books did was make me very concerned that Vivi was going to one day grow up to be a DJ at techno raves. She enjoyed hearing the same sounds over and over and over; she couldn't push the same button fast enough to get that sound going again. And again. And again. I see glow sticks in her future.

Even when we got to books with real stories, the point of the books was completely lost on my child. Viv would hand me a book with a semblance of a plot, and I'd pull her up onto my lap, ready to embark on a journey of the mind, to share a story of words and pictures and—BAM!—she would close the book on my thumb and wiggle off my lap in search of some Tupperware to put on her head. There were a lot of stories that went like this: "Once there were two little bears who lived—the end!"

As she got older, Vivi began to show more interest in getting past the first page, but she still didn't have time to dilly-dally with much before turning the page. This forced me to go off script and make up stories on the fly as she sped the plot along with her surprisingly strong baby hands. These stories went a little like this: "There are two bears. Their mom is mad. Their room is messy. Dad has an idea. They clean up. The end!"

Soon she progressed to spending more time on each page but preferred to spend that time simply pointing at the different details in the pictures, despite my best efforts to interest her in the words written on the page. Story time then went like this: "Two little bears, up in their room. Mommy says—yes, that's a doggy. Mommy says—and that's a shoe, two shoes, and a ball on the floor, and toys and a trophy and, yes, let's turn the page. A messy, messy room. What are the bears to do? Mommy is—yes, mommy is wearing a hat, and shoes. And there is a bird outside the window and . . ." These story-telling adventures resembled the inner monologue of a hyperactive person on uppers.

The key to finding a good book is finding one with juuust the right amount of text on each page. Too little text and you (read: I) will get angry that there is actually a "written by" credit on the front of the book. Too much text and you will have to jump ship halfway through the page to keep the child interested, creating holes in an already flimsy plot. It's a precarious tightrope dance that involves balancing a baby, performing Broadway-caliber renditions of ridiculous stories, and more than the occasional zoo animal in formal attire. It ain't for the weak, that's for sure.

As I sit here writing all these words about children's books, I realize I've just written enough words to fill 24,562,435 books for kids. So I'm done with you adults—I'm moving on to another genre. I present to you my first book for children. I wrote it from the heart, and I dedicate it to Vivian, who has taught me about the things that really matter in this life. It's called *Give Me Your $7.95*; I hope you like it. It has been a labor of love. And, coincidentally, it took less time to write than my actual labor experience.

Give me your
$7.95

A rhyming, touch and feel,
123, ABC book with
accurately drawn animals

Story and Illustrations by: Dawn Dais
(She's very talented)

A is for apple
And here you see there's two
Isn't this so exciting?
And it's educating you

How to count past 10
Is nothing you need to know
That's why kids books only go that high
Cause math is mainly for show.

B is for Bee
Yes, a letter and a bug
You might as well learn now
The English language is no fun

Just in case you were wondering
Yes, bug rhymes with fun
Trust me on these things
I'm an expert rhymer

C is for Crocodile,
As anyone should know
I wouldn't want to draw a Cat
Because you've actually seen one befo'

If I draw pictures of animals
That you have never seen
You won't know I'm a horrible drawer
And won't make fun of me

Now I will show you a mouse
Because aren't they so much fun
Until Mommy sees one in the kitchen
And screams at the top of her lungs

This mouse hangs out with a bear
They are the same size as you can tell
If you happen to see one in the woods
You should probably run like hell

And now we're on the moon
Because why not really
Touch right here and feel
Yes, the moon feels like paper silly

We've learned oh so much
During this special time
I think we can all agree
I've earned your $7.95

15

SINGLE PARENTS KICK ASS

The more I wade through this parenting gig, the more respect I have for single parents. They kick a tremendous amount of ass. Even though I'm sure it rarely feels that way to them.

If you are heading into single parenthood and are wondering what you have in store, look through the other chapters of this book, then multiply them by about four, maybe six. It's going to be hard. But you're going to kick the crap out of it. Babies have a way of coming on the scene and dropping a bomb in the middle of their parent's life. And somehow, no matter how many parents there are, we just figure out how to navigate around all the new rubble and learn how to build it into something sturdy for our kids. Single parents have all the tools they need for the construction.

I talked to three of my MOFLs, Channing, Karen, and Jodi, about their experiences as single moms and the unique struggles that come from tackling parenting alone. Channing is a single mom by choice to twin boys, Karen became a single mom after a surprise pregnancy, and Jodi broke up with her daughter's father in the baby's first year. All three women have 100 percent custody of their kids; Karen and Jodi receive a small amount in child support.

I recently had the thought that if someone was single before having a baby, the jolt into parenthood would be even greater than the one I experienced. Being in a relationship had eased me into the idea of being responsible to another human being, and that was a big adjustment for someone who had been single for most of her adult life. Just having to think about someone else in my day-to-day plans had been a big change of pace. Obviously I had responsibilities to other people before I was in a relationship, but none of those people required quite as much consideration as a partner does. Adding another, much tinier, more high-maintenance person to the mix was jarring, but I was already accustomed to a world that revolved around more than just me. I can only imagine how many adjustments would be going on if a person went from being single and free to completely responsible for a tiny human around the clock.

Karen agreed: "Yes, it was a shock!! I went from complete freedom and not having to answer to anyone to complete lockdown. Remember, as a single mom I don't even have the luxury of easily running to the store if I run out of diapers. I have to bundle up the baby and taking her with me. For me, that was the hardest part. Not the loss of going out with friends for drinks, just the need to now plan ahead for my every move and be less carefree in my day-to-day life."

Karen said the first three months were the hardest for her, and she has the internet to thank for her survival. "I relied a lot on online ordering EVERYTHING. I even grocery-shopped online. I only went out when I had to."

Like any new mom, single moms need a lot of help from friends and family. Do not hesitate to set up help in advance and accept help from those who offer. Even if they just want to drop off a meal, it will save you time and energy. Once they get there with the food, you can try to wrestle them inside and throw the baby at them while you go take a nap for an hour. It's worth a shot.

Channing recommends getting out in front of those difficult first months by putting a plan in place well before you give birth: "My mantra is that it's easier to cancel help you don't need than to secure extra help when you're at your wit's end. Right before and right after delivery, people are super-excited to sign up and help, so I used Meal Train Plus to set up people to help with food and other appointments. I even created undefined helping slots so I could decide what help I needed on short notice."

When I asked my MOFLs what advice they would give other single moms who are just starting out, they shared some habits that have helped them along.

Channing is big on structure. "Set a routine and stick with it. Without a partner you don't have the same 'backstop' if you wear yourself out, so it's harder to roll with things. The sooner you can develop a routine, the easier it will be. Tell people no if it's going to disrupt your schedule."

Jodi thinks it's important to stay rested. "I would recommend trying to sleep whenever you can, because you will find yourself exhausted all the time with no one there to help relieve you."

Karen is always willing to say yes to helping hands. "I accept any and all help from family and friends. That's really the key. It totally takes a village to raise a child as a single parent. As soon as I realized that and started asking for help, life got a little easier."

I also asked my single moms about what I see could be one of the plus sides of single parenting: not having to consult anyone else on your parenting decisions. The women agreed that there is definitely an advantage to being the final and only word on important decisions and discipline, but they saw some downsides as well.

"Yes, there is value in making all the decisions, but that also leaves a level of stress on your shoulders because you have no one to talk to about whether it is the right choice or not," Jodi says. "It's nice to be able to make a decision and move forward on it without worrying about getting approval, though."

Karen agrees: "I second-guess myself a little more (I think) because I don't have anyone else as a sounding board who is as invested in my daughter as I am."

But Karen sees that there is an advantage to only one parent disciplining. "My daughter is not confused by two different types or levels of discipline, which I see a lot in a couple's dynamics. She knows what she is going to get from me and knows she can't run to Dad for another answer."

But what happens when Mom is the one who wants to run? "The downside of this is that there are moments when I need a break! In the middle of a tantrum, I just need to walk away. In a couple's environment, it's that time when the other parent can step in while the overheated one can step away and gain composure. Unfortunately, this can't happen with me, so it gets difficult. I have literally had to walk out of the room and take a breather."

This leads to how single moms manage to juggle all of life's requirements. There are jobs and groceries and housework and doctor's appointments and playdates and homework. And just one person to pull it all off. Jodi seems to have a strategy similar to mine. "I manage everything by flying by the seat of my pants. We have a pretty good routine for work, daycare, and evenings, so we just go through the motions."

Karen has figured out a way to balance her work and child. "Yes, I work sixty-plus hours a week, and my daughter is in daycare after school, but my phone and laptop are not on while my daughter is awake. I like the fact that she sees that I do go to work and have a good job. I think it's a good example for a girl."

All three moms have great support from their parents, which allows them a little flexibility in scheduling work events and travel. If you are single and have a good relationship with your parents (or even just an okay relationship), I highly recommend living near them once your baby arrives. Channing's mom moved in with her to help when the twins were babies, and Karen and Jodi both rely heavily on their parents for support.

Jodi has arranged for her daughter to stay over at Grandma's house once a week so Mommy can get up and go to the gym one morning. It's a little thing, but Jodi loves those free mornings to herself to meet up with a gym buddy, work out for twenty minutes, and chat at Starbucks for forty minutes. Mama needs a little Starbucks now and then, you know. (Side note: You might be officially old if going to Starbucks sounds like more fun than going out for drinks.)

Also, like Karen, try to get to a place where you are comfortable asking for and accepting help from friends. You are woman, hear you roar, but sometimes you are a woman who needs a last-minute babysitter. Building a supportive community around you will not only be good for you; it will also provide your child with an extended family that will give him or her comfort over the years.

More than anything, remember that you have everything your child needs to thrive. "Go easy on yourself," says Jodi. "All your baby needs is love, and as a single parent you can provide that."

16

HAVING PETS DID NOT PREPARE YOU FOR THIS

(crate training is not an option,
so take that off your registry)

	PETS	vs.	KIDS
ACTUALLY COME WHEN YOU SAY "COME HERE."	91 percent of the time (100 percent of the time if you also say, "Treat")		4 percent of the time (0 percent of the time if you are in public)
THEIR RESPONSE TO YOU BEING SICK AND/OR HUNGOVER	"Let's sleep all day!"		"Don't care. Give me boob."
LEASHES	Acceptable (although not often needed)		Unacceptable (although often needed)
WHAT THEIR CRYING MEANS	They are hurt		They are hurt, hungry, full, tired, gassy, hot, cold, or colicky. Or, they just feel like crying.
WHAT THEIR CRIES SOUND LIKE	Cute little whimpers		Wails that make the neighbors question your parenting and overall humanity

How having a pet prepares you for children:

- Helps build a tolerance for another being's excrement. (Although if you don't want to deal with it, you cannot just pretend your kid didn't poop and keep on walking.)

- Petco will teach you about stores dedicated to overpriced, unnecessary items that you will be convinced you cannot live without.

- Both make spontaneous travel plans impossible. (Trying to leave your child in a kennel for the weekend is frowned upon.)

One night late in my pregnancy, Chipper Jen texted me to say that when she sees young couples partying it up, she laaaaughs at how their lives will change once they have kids. It was 9:30 at night, and she was going to bed because she was so exhausted. At the time we had a kitten who thought that jumping on us at 3:00 a.m. and playing a fast and furious game of tag with the four posts of the bed was a fantastic way to pass the early-morning hours. I texted Jen back, saying that I was totally prepared for parenting because the damn cat was waking me up every night anyway.

I wasn't being sarcastic.

I think back on that text at least once a day now and just shake my head at my own naivete. I also thought about it roughly 53,452 times a day the first few months of my child's life. Sometimes I'd tilt my head and let out a hearty "Bwahahahahpffthsst!" But most of the time head tilting was beyond my energy level, so a simple snort was all I could muster.

Before I got pregnant, when I was having difficulty getting pregnant, we walked into a PetSmart for dog food on Kitten Adoption Day and walked out with three little homeless kitties. This made for a grand total of two dogs and five cats under our care. I'm sure this happens a lot, actually: women or couples are at that place where they are ready for a baby, but a baby isn't coming, so they stock up on pets to be the lucky recipients of that heightened maternal instinct. They probably think, like I did, that having animals will prepare them for when the baby finally arrives.

Bwahahahahpffthsst!

Now, don't get me wrong. I do think that having a pet is a step in the right direction and everyone who is thinking about having a kid should get a dog first and see if they can actually keep it alive for a year before bringing a tiny human home. I remember when I got my first puppy I lived by myself in a condo. I got a Pomeranian because one of my cousins had a Pomeranian, and all that dog did was sit next to me on the couch all day when I took care of him (ahhhh, days of yore, when I spent hours on the couch . . .). He was like a little stuffed animal that needed to be fed every once in a while. I thought all Poms were like that and was SHOCKED when I got my puppy home, put him next to me on the couch, and he promptly jumped off and started running around the condo barking like his tail was on fire (or like he was a Pomeranian, it turns out). I had a similar wake-up call when I got my newborn home, and to my shock and awe she didn't just "sleep and eat" the way so many people had told me she would.

My simple, carefree, single life was cramped a bit by the addition of a puppy, especially adding a puppy to a condo with no backyard. I had to get up in the middle of the night to let him out to pee, I had to hire someone to come during the middle of the day while I was at work to let him out to pee, and I couldn't stay out for hours and days at a time because I had to get home so he could pee. Basically, his urine dictated all my plans.

That kind of responsibility definitely gets you ready for the changes that will come when you have a kid, but nothing can really prepare you for the wonders that await when you are responsible for an actual human person. First of all, the worst-case scenario for not getting up in the middle of the night with my puppy or not hiring someone to come let him out during the day was that I was going to have pee on my floor. By contrast, the worst-case scenario for not taking care of my baby was that Child Protective Services would pay me a visit. If I left my dog alone at home for hours on end, I would feel really guilty about it, but if I left my kid at home alone, I'd feel really incarcerated. And unlike my solution to the hyperactive kitten, I quickly found that simply locking the crying baby out of the room and going back to sleep was not a viable option. All of my training was for naught, I quickly discovered.

People who don't have kids often make claims that they love their animals as much as parents love their children. The term "fur baby" is thrown around a lot to illustrate this idea (or perhaps to illustrate really hairy kids? I'm not sure). I get it, before I had my baby I couldn't imagine loving anything more than I did my sweet, innocent pets. I now know that I was wrong, but not for simple reasons. Pet owners love their pets *because* they are cute and loyal and fun and bring joy and light into their lives. However, parents love their children for all the above reasons but continue to love them *despite the fact* that they are demanding and exhausting and smelly and freedom ending. It's just simple science that you have to love your children more than you love your pets (or anything else on the planet for that matter—ahem, sleep)—because if you didn't, you might actually call Child Protective Services yourself and request a pickup.

Even though you will love your child more than you love your pets, if you are anything like me you'll also come to *really* appreciate your animals during those first months with a new baby. Sure, I have to feed my animals and pick up their poop, but in exchange they greet me with the enthusiasm of an Oprah's Favorite Things audience member EVERY TIME I come home (sometimes if I just walk back in from getting the mail). They will gladly lie in bed with me all day while I watch TV and eat pizza (in fact they prefer that schedule), they are down for a road trip at the drop of a hat (no packing required), and (most important) they do not have the ability to shriek at the top of their lungs. They are a simple bunch and are endlessly satisfied as long as they get some food and a belly rub every day.

So, make sure you don't forget about your animals in those first few months with a newborn. There was a time when those pets were your babies, and there is no way they can really understand why they have been relegated down to the status of a mere animal ("How dare you!") after years of first dibs on your lap. I try to give all my animals a little extra love when the baby isn't around, often right before bed or in the morning before the kid wakes up. In those moments, when they are snuggling their little noses into my neck, I always flash back to when it was just me and my hyperactive puppy in that little condo. I remember how hard it was to adjust to the responsibility of a pet but how much it taught me about my capacity to love another being. I think, *I figured out the pet thing, so in no time at all I'll get this kid dialed in, and it will be smooth sailing.* At that point all the animals let out a "Bwahahahahpffthsst!" then roll over onto their backs and demand a belly rub before the baby wakes up and steals their thunder yet again.

Quite a few of my MOFLs have pets now and had pets before their kids came along. Pretty much all of them (even the veterinarian) made it abundantly clear that they don't think pets prepare you for children at all. Although Erika did point out that her weak-bladdered cat made her a lot more tolerant of her child when he arrived. She says, "My lovely 'pee anywhere I want, whenever I want' kitty definitely taught me a lot about patience, and I know Luke has benefited from my now Zen-like state in regard to messes."

I have to agree that the main benefit to owning a pet before owning a child is the forced interaction with another being's poop, pee, and puke. One has to build up a tolerance for such things, and an animal is an excellent way to ease in. If I hadn't been exposed to so much foul-smelling excrement in advance, I don't think I would have survived my child's first weeks without passing out from some of the smells and visuals she provided. (See Chapter 13, "Poop, Puke, and Pee.")

When asked about the benefits of having animals around children, it was also pretty unanimously believed that animals were beneficial to and generally adorable around kids. Dana, mother of two children and four pets, mentioned a study that found babies in homes with pets are healthier on the whole than children in pet-free homes (no, fish do not count). I read about the study and it seems that researchers aren't really sure why having dogs results in healthier babies, but they think it might have something to do with babies building up immunity through the germs that animals bring around. I'm glad to hear fancy scientists support that theory, because it is the one I repeated to myself over and over every time I wasn't quick enough to stop one of the animals from licking the baby right in her mouth while she giggled and gladly opened up for more.

All the moms also agreed that our own independent studies prove that there is nothing cuter on this planet than babies with animals (a close second is teenagers with animals, because they can walk them while you stay in the house watching TV). My heart would absolutely melt every time one of my animals curled up next to the nursing baby or tolerated her pulling its tail a *liiiitle* too hard. And you can't help but think you are ingraining some positive qualities when you see how kind your little person can be to her pets (tail pulling notwithstanding).

Chipper Jen points out that having dogs around as the kids get older is a plus from a cleaning standpoint as well. I can vouch for that. The amount of baby-flung food that parents have to pick up off the floor seems like reason enough to go adopt a pooch immediately. Even when we are out at a restaurant, both Vivian and I look down for the dogs when she throws something on the ground. It's crossed my mind a few times to go out to dinner with the puppies in tow.

I will say that despite the great benefits of having animals around your kids, it definitely adds a lot of extra work. Sometimes the added insanity of pets is juuuuust enough to push you over into the crazy sauce. One night, while Becky and I were both lying on couches in the living room, watching the child playing peacefully with her toys by herself, the dogs WOULD NOT stop jumping up and down, barking, whining, and otherwise driving us insane. My other half, at her wit's end, finally yelled, "When are these dogs supposed to die?!!" It was, admittedly, a horrible thing to say but a good example of how thin you are stretched when you are balancing life, work, children, and animals. Of course, she doesn't want the dogs to die (mostly because, after yelling that question, she would have to live forever with the thought that she willed their demise), but sometimes everything we're juggling does seem like a lot. And, unfortunately for her, we picked breeds that tend to live a long time.

To help alleviate the chaos, we simply gave the child a cup of her crunchy snacks, which she threw one by one on the floor for her suddenly calm dogs. An entertained kid, happy dogs, and resting parents? BAM! We got this! (Also, we are going to need a Costco-size package of crunchy snacks, to keep everyone entertained for the next five years.)

17

WHO NEEDS A HEALTH PLAN WHEN YOU HAVE THE INTERNET?

(medical school is overrated)

An equation:

Paranoid + Hours on = A Pediatrician's
Mother   the   Worst
                 Internets   Nightmare

A small sampling of internet forum acronyms:

BD—Baby Dance (Sex—it's only one more letter; why not just use the actual word?)

CM—Cervical Mucus (Please, no.)

CP—Cervical Position (Who knew there was more than one position? The internet. That's who knew.)

DD—Dear Daughter / **DS**—Dear Son (If you're searching for help on the internet, they might not be acting so "dear.")

EWCM—Egg-White Cervical Mucus (Even more no.)

FMU—First Morning Urine (Also a great name for an alternative rock band.)

LO—Little One (The word "baby" is too complicated?)

TMI—Too Much Information (Exactly.)

The good news:
Every disease is described on the internet.

The bad news:
There are often accompanying photos.

During my first frantic weeks home with the baby, any time I ran into a parenting question I would text Chipper Jen, call my mom, and search the internet in rapid succession. If you don't have a Chipper Jen or a mom like my mom in your life, you will quickly become reliant on Google as your go-to source for information.

With Google at your fingertips, you won't need silly things like health insurance and doctors. There is nothing that will pop up regarding baby care that isn't covered in great detail on at least 3,528 different internet forums. With a little digging and common sense, you are sure to find your answer. Although you are also sure to go screaming into the night after the internet convinces you your child has contracted several known and unknown untreatable illnesses. So proceed with caution.

If you are going to venture onto the interweb (and believe me, with the amount of free time you will have with a baby hanging off your boob, you are going to venture onto the interweb), be sure to set some ground rules.

First, do not freak out after reading one message board or comment section response about a lady who had a friend with a cousin whose kid died from the EXACT symptom you are searching. Always read plenty of different sites before freaking out. And even then, call your version of Chipper Jen, your mom, and/or your doctor to confirm it's actually freak-out time.

Second, get to know the acronyms that are commonly used on these different forums (see some of my favorites on the previous page). Reading message boards without knowing what the many acronyms stand for can be a bit like reading redacted government documents and trying to piece together what the author was really trying to say. Of course, once you realize all the weird things that have been granted an acronym, you may realize that the acronyms were there to protect your poor eyes.

Third, and most important, do NOT get involved in online forums, most especially online forum debates. Women are crazy. Moms are crazier. Moms on the internet are the craziest of all. Do not engage, back away slowly, and move on to another site if you start feeling the urge to participate.

In addition to answers I also find a lot of comfort on the internet. Somehow my mind is put at ease when I enter my particular struggle and find 134,623,462 sites about that topic. This means that, unlike I had suspected, I am not the only parent in the history of parents to deal with this particular issue. Knowing this helps calm me and makes me realize none of us know what the hell we are doing, and that none of us have a problem telling the internet all about our ineptitude.

While it's always a good idea to consult your health professional with questions, I often found the advice nurses had very little to offer me in the way of real advice. First, they would try to determine whether my child was in a dire situation. Once that possibility was eliminated, they would read from a script of recommended comments based on the symptoms I described. Sometimes they would tell me to come in to see the doctor, but just like your car at the auto shop, your kid will work just fine when in the actual doctor's office. (Side note: Take videos with your phone of any troubling symptoms your child may have. Do not assume the child will show any of these symptoms when in the actual doctor's office or that you will be able to reenact the symptoms yourself when explaining to the doctor.)

After dealing with an advice nurse with no real advice, you can head over to the internet to hear straight from moms' mouths about what did or didn't work for them. There are usually 14,000 solutions to each issue, but that's okay. Because in my opinion it's never a bad idea to have a backup plan (or 13,999).

The internet, in addition to providing detailed cures for all ailments and problems, can also save you the hassle of having to be a functional member of society. Instead of ever leaving your house, you can just visit the internet and order all the diaper and baby goods you need to survive. BuyBuyBaby.com or Amazon.com are especially fun sites, because after you hit Purchase, your order arrives on your doorstep about 3.5 minutes later. I'm not sure how they do it, but their delivery time (with free shipping!) is ridiculous. And a godsend when you are one bad poop away from an extreme diaper shortage situation.

Other sites, like BabyCenter.com and TheBump.com, offer newsletter sign-ups on their sites. You enter the birth date of your baby, and like magic the sites will send you emails about what is going on with your child based on his or her age. I always find these updates scary accurate, to the point where I will be bemoaning one of Vivian's newest challenges and an email will pop up that day telling me all about how to deal with it. I take comfort in these emails, knowing that whatever we are dealing with is very age appropriate and most likely has an expiration date that will hopefully arrive soon.

That said, I'd caution you about getting too wrapped up in the expected milestone and development benchmarks. In the early days of parenthood, I would study those benchmarks like they were an arrival time for a plane. I'd just be sitting at the milestone airport, usually early, because I was so ready for the milestone to get here, waiting for my kid to arrive as scheduled. When her plane was delayed or detoured, I would get increasingly impatient with her and all the books / email newsletters that promised certain time frames.

But babies will do what they want, when they want. So will older kids. And without a doubt so will teens. It's best you get used to it now. Communicate with your pediatrician about your baby's development, so they can catch anything alarming. But other than that, let the kid arrive on their own schedule. And stop beating yourself up if things aren't happening on the exact same schedule as other babies you may know.

In other tech news, I recommend loading up on baby-centric apps to make parenting easier. Before you even head to the hospital, you should have a baby-tracking app that lets you track anything and everything the baby is doing. The hospital will provide you with an old-school piece of paper for this task, but your memory becomes useless the second a child pops out of you, so you're going to need the help of technology to survive this time. Baby-tracking apps (there are several) let you time how long you've breastfed, which boob you used last, how many wet and poopy diapers the baby had, and how long the kid slept. These are all things that the pediatrician is going to want to know, and all things that will leave your brain 1.2 seconds after they happen.

If you are like me, you thrive on order and a semblance of control. And, unfortunately, babies are notorious for not participating in either of those things. But baby-tracking apps can at least give you a small glimmer of order by allowing you to record necessary facts and times, and storing them for you safely away from your useless brain and unorganized house. When I got Vivian home, my baby-tracking apps were the only place that I felt organized. Look! A graph! A color-coded table! I'm not sure I really needed a color-coded table, but I did need something besides my memory to hold baby facts, and these apps stepped up to the plate to fortify my hobbled brain cells.

So go on, dear mamas, and brave the wide, wide world of the internet and technology. For there you will find answers and acronyms and weird photos galore. Can you think of a better way to pass the time while you have a baby hanging from your boob? I think not.

18

YOU'LL NEVER SLEEP AGAIN

(dark circles will become a permanent accessory)

Sleep aids my kid has needed since her birth	vs.	Sleep aids I've needed since my kid's birth
1. Rocking		1. Closed eyes*
2. Swinging		2. Being horizontal*
		(*optional)
3. Boobs		
4. Bottle		
5. Blanket		
6. Stuffed Animal		
7. Vibration		
8. Noise Machine		
9. Music		
10. Night Light		
11. Fan		
12. Back Rub		
13. Forehead Rub		
14. Lullaby		
15. Baby Doll		
16. Car Ride		

The ways to ruin a child by sleep training:

METHOD	HOW YOU DO IT	LONG-TERM EFFECT
CRY IT OUT	Baby cries inside crib. Parents cry in hallway.	Child grows up with abandonment issues and the need to weep before sleep.
NO TEARS	Comfort the baby before a tear has fallen.	Child will need a nighttime bottle and rocker until age twenty-seven.
COSLEEPING	Baby sleeps in bed with parents.	Teenager still sleeping in bed with parents.
BABYWISE	Get the baby on an eat/play/sleep schedule.	An adult who can barely keep her eyes open at a dinner party after the games are played.

It is important that you adequately prepare yourself mentally for the fact that once you have a child you are doomed to a life of no sleep. And then go ahead and realize that there is no adequate way to prepare for this situation.

In the weeks before my baby arrived, I slept as much as humanly possible. When I woke up in the morning, I did not get out of bed; I simply answered emails on my phone, made a few calls, then took a brunch-time nap. When my partner would give me a hard time about my laziness, I would inform her of the unfortunate math that was coming my way: A baby needs to eat every three hours when it is brand new. And rumor around town was that I was going to be the source of my baby's eating. I didn't like where this was headed as far as my sleep was concerned. All I knew for sure was that until that baby actually needed my boobs, I was going to relax with them as much as possible.

Somehow in my mind this meant that I was going to be all rested up and ready to go when the child arrived, as if there were a place in my body that stores up excess sleep to be used when I hit a short supply. (Side note: Dear scientists of the world, let's skip over all that silly cancer research and get on figuring out how to store up sleep!) Unfortunately, my plan didn't work quite as well as I had imagined it would. By the time my baby was two days old, I was already beyond exhausted and had dark circles under my eyes that looked nearly painted on.

As the days wore on (and wore on me), the lack of sleep turned into official sleep deprivation. You'll know you've officially become sleep deprived when you have the unique feeling of being drunk, high, and on a psychiatric hold all at the same time. Some call this "time for a straitjacket," but we'll just call it "new motherhood."

Unfortunately, your only hope of ever walking through your days with anything other than a blank stare and a tangled ponytail on top of your head is convincing your child to sleep. And preferably to sleep at night, for longer than four hours at a time. This means you are going to have to sleep-train the little one.

After you inevitably try yelling at the top of your lungs, "Go to sleep!!!" you'll need to move on to an actual sleep-training plan. Although if you have a fussier baby, yelling, "Go to sleep!!!" might actually prove as effective as some of the more structured plans.

There are countless books and websites out there that go into great detail about the different ways to get your child to sleep like a real human being. You will come across most of this information when you are frantically searching for "make my baby sleep" on Google at two in the morning. And three in the morning. And four...

When we first got the baby home, she had no idea what the whole day/night thing was about. She would sleep all day and party all night. This is a common thing for little ones, so our biggest goal was to get her to understand that nighttime was in fact for sleeping, not crying or playing. We would make her room dark and quiet, to let her know it was time to sleep. She would have her eyes open wide in our arms, wondering where all the light went. We would put her in her swing, but she was so small that even the lowest setting seemed like it was going to throw her out and across the room.

Eventually I discovered that if I walked around with her and bounced her a little she would settle down a bit. I imagined this felt sort of like being in my belly. I told the pediatrician, "She does okay if I walk around shaking her a bit. I think it's comforting." The doctor did not enjoy my using the word "shaking." "Well, we don't recommend shaking a baby, ever." "Well, obviously, but it does calm her down, so there's that."

Once Vivian got situated with her days and nights (this probably took a few days, but honestly I remember it as weeks and weeks of time), we needed to implement a real sleep-training plan. Initially I had hoped to do the Babywise method of sleep training, because I had heard wonderful things from parents who had successfully Babywised their babies. The basic idea is that you feed your baby every three to four hours (depending on their age) and implement an eat/play/sleep schedule from the very beginning. Your baby's days are very scheduled out, and this can be a wonderful thing, especially for parents who already have kids or who just want more structure to their days.

The baby wakes up at a certain time every day (or you wake them up), you feed them, you play with them, and then they go back to sleep. Then you repeat throughout the day. I tried to implement this strategy when Vivian was a couple of weeks old. But she wasn't really on board. Her biggest problem? She really, really enjoyed a good nap after a good meal, which made the "play" part difficult to execute. This is pretty common for little ones, so some Babywise moms recommended making efforts to keep her awake while feeding. This involved constantly stroking her throughout her meal, to remind her to wake up, and wiping a cold washcloth on her to shock her into staying awake. Being as though my child was born with my excellent napping DNA, she was undeterred.

One friend suggested giving the baby a bath right after feeding her to wake her up for playtime. Vivian slept through the bath. They also recommended using the cold washcloth after feeding, to shock her awake. I did this once, holding the sleeping, full baby on my lap while I ran a cold washcloth over her body. This worked, but it shocked her so much that she woke up and spit up all over me. Somehow shocking a sleeping new baby into vomiting seemed very cruel to me, and I couldn't bring myself to do it again. We still tried to stick to a general three-hour feeding schedule, but other than that we were BabyNotSoSmart.

After our Babywise debacle, we went an easier route. That route included letting the child nurse until she was asleep and then laying her down in her crib to slumber. This is what would be considered a No-Cry method. It seemed easier at the time because my boob did all the work for me. However, in the long run I think it probably ended up doing more harm than good—for us. That's because eventually Vivian stopped falling into a hard sleep on my boob and would wake up as soon as I put her down.

That's when we moved over to a Cry-It-Out method. The crying came from all members of the family. If Vivian started crying when I put her in her crib, I would simply tell her it was okay and that it was bedtime, and I would leave the room. Then I would sit in the hallway holding her monitor and a timer, waiting a certain amount of time before going back in. This process was gut wrenching, but it did work after a few days. She never went straight down with no fuss, but it eventually took only one trip in and out of the room before she calmed herself down.

We did, however, make a huge error in rocking her with a bedtime bottle for way too long. When we finally weaned her off the milk, bedtime got moved back an hour because she just wouldn't fall asleep without her bottle to soothe her in advance. She would lie in her crib with her eyes wide open forever before slipping off to sleep. She continues to play and talk for a good hour in bed before finally settling in. Apparently she needs to sum up the day to her stuffed animal before they can sleep.

One thing we absolutely never tried, because I was totally against it, was cosleeping. Sometimes, during really tough nights, my partner would pick up the baby and try to bring her into our bed, hoping that solution would give us all a chance to sleep. I would instantly hop up, grab the baby, and head back to the nursery. I have heard horror stories of trying to get older kids (from five to ten years old) out of their parents' bed, and I refused to even start down that road. Plus there was just no way I was ever going to sleep soundly if I knew the baby was in the bed. I would be afraid of rolling on her, her rolling off the bed, or one of us suffocating her with our comforter. I already had roughly eight million ways my child could suffer harm running through my brain; I didn't need to add more to the mix.

The biggest thing to remember, no matter what method you choose, is patience. Patience with the baby, patience with your partner, patience with yourself. The sleeping thing won't happen overnight, and all the nights before it happens will be difficult. Communicate with your partner, and make sure you two are on the same page as to how you will be tackling this undertaking. Trying to get a child to sleep *and* battling with your spouse will make for the most unpleasant of nighttime rituals.

Also, try not to slip into a deep depression if you hear other parents talking about what great sleepers their babies are. Like everything else having to do with children, every kid will take to sleeping a little bit differently. Eventually your baby will get there, too.

I asked my MOFLs what they did in an effort to get their children to sleep regularly.

Sarah had more luck Babywising her kids than I did. "I followed Babywise and it worked! Jake slept eight hours without waking at five weeks (consistently by twelve weeks), Theo at eight weeks, and Bea at eight weeks. They're all still great sleepers and nappers. The longest we let one of them cry was thirty minutes (two nights and never woke again), and the others never needed to cry it out."

Show-off.

Amy also wants us to feel bad. "We didn't do anything special, but we are fortunate that both our girls are good sleepers. They both were sleeping through the night at two months old."

Erika didn't have it as easy. "At about the nine-month mark I was about to lose my mind because Luke was still waking up to nurse four to five times a night. We started letting him cry it out, which was agonizing at first, but after only a few days he slept 'like a baby' for around eleven hours a night. It was incredible. His entire demeanor shifted pretty dramatically right after he started sleeping continuously through the night. He was much, much happier in general. Clearly the poor kiddo just needed me to stop hovering so he could get some good sleep!"

Sommer, mom of one, also hit her breaking point. "Well, after going up and down the stairs fifteen times a night, we finally hired a 'Ferberizer' nanny (we were DESPERATE) at six months old. She was only here one night, and we never had a problem again."

The only thing more challenging than getting a baby to go to sleep can be getting them to *stay* asleep. God have mercy on any UPS deliveryman, gardener, or dog who makes a noise while a baby is sleeping. I'm actually surprised that I made it through my child's first year without committing a felony as a result of an unsuspecting visitor nearly waking the baby. If I had had more energy, I'm not sure what I would have been capable of.

I asked my moms for any tricks they used to keep their babies sleeping soundly, and you will see I'm not the only one who was a little kookoo. Erika swaddled her poor boy to within an inch of his life. "Swaddling seemed to help Luke sleep, but it would never stay tight enough for long, so I started using a belt crisscrossed around the swaddle. That seemed to work pretty well until I started freaking out about the belt accidentally slipping and suffocating him. I stopped using the belt immediately (obviously), and Luke went back to only sleeping while lying on my chest or my husband's. Then we found the Miracle Blanket. It truly was miraculous."

Sarah went the auditory route. "We had what we fondly called 'Baby Crack.' I downloaded a vacuum cleaner on iTunes and had it playing repeatedly next to her bouncy, in the stroller, wherever she was!"

Chipper Jen's kid liked to move, shockingly enough. "Austin loved the swing! I'm pretty sure he napped in the swing till he was eighteen months!"

Amy had a very dry baby. "I would turn on the hair dryer and hold it in one hand, the baby in the other arm. It was magic. I would tell my husband, 'I'm gonna go blow dry Kenny.'"

Jenine knows someone who *really* needed to sleep. "I have a friend who spent a ton of money on a pair of fake arms. Her son would only sleep in her arms at night, so these things were supposed to replace you somehow. I love to tease her about this, but then I spent almost one hundred dollars on a potty-training doll in a moment of desperation!"

Sometimes I feel like parenting itself is just one moment of desperation after another, with all of us frantically trying to figure out the answers as we go along. If the "baby crack" and "blow drying the baby" adventures above teach you anything, it's that none of us have any idea what we are doing. We all count on one another and the internet and plain dumb luck to help us figure out what will work.

So be patient with your child and yourself as you figure out your special sleeping recipe. But you might want to call in an order for a pair of fake arms right now, just to be on the safe side.

PARTNER CORNER: SLEEP DEPRIVATION

Pat: It's really bad. Sleep deprivation can ruin relationships. You need to sleep-train your baby. When the baby is asleep, it's the only time you and your partner will be able to have normal conversations. Also, you will hate every single person that makes noise while your baby sleeps. "Don't wake the baby" is the new mantra in your household.

Larry: Being in the military I thought I was used to sleep deprivation. I actually rolled my eyes with the lack of sleep everyone was warning me about. The wife and I had a plan: sleep when the baby was asleep during the day and at night we would alternate. I imagine the universe laughed at me when it heard that plan. It was impossible for my wife to sleep during the day because there was so much to be done that can't be done with an awake baby. And at night we would both wake up every time the baby did.

I became so tired that one time when my wife asked me to go get something from the kitchen I stood up, turned to face her while she was talking, and woke up to her saying my name. I had fallen back asleep while kneeling against the edge of the bed. And that wasn't the end of the episode. Not three minutes later I scared my mother-in-law who was headed to the bathroom and found me asleep slouched, upright against the hallway wall.

19

YOUR HOUSE IS WAY TOO SMALL

(or Hurricane Baby is way too big)

Where you spent most of your time entertaining pre-baby	vs.	Where you spend most of your time entertaining post-baby
Living room, dining room, kitchen, backyard		The floor

How YOUR HOUSE is like a FRAT HOUSE:

- Dishes piled in the sink because the occupants are too lazy to do them.

- Lots of puking after drinking too much from bottles.

- Your mom and dad come by to drop off real meals every once in a while.

- Incoherent young people crying at all hours of the night.

- Piles of unopened informative books lying around.

- Underwear (diapers) strewn about.

- One or more people likely to be sleeping on the couch in the middle of the day.

- Everyone in the house looking hungover.

- Hand-me-down items make up most of the prominent decor.

- Adults often wear the same clothes day after day, despite a growing number of stains/smells.

Something happens right around the time you get home from your baby shower, and it is irreversible. At that point, after you unload the last of the adorable adorableness that you received at your shower, you will look around your house and say, "I swear this space used to seem bigger."

And it did. Before your little one is even here, he or she will occupy every square foot of your living space (and even some wall space as well). You wouldn't think such a tiny little being (especially one not even born yet) could take up so much room, but you would be so, so, so, so wrong. Because this being comes accessorized to the hilt.

Before your child arrives you will accumulate every baby must-have, can't-live-without item for sale in stores or online. Some call this "nesting"; others call it "preparing for battle." You cram those items into all the different corners of your house during your pregnancy while also accepting gifts and hand-me-downs from all who offer. Then your house starts to resemble an opening montage of the show *Hoarders*, with closets packed to the gills, whatnots piled on must-haves.

We had a room in the house that was the baby's room before and after she arrived. For nine months I would just open the door to the room, throw baby stuff in, then shut it quickly so as to avoid dealing with the growing chaos. By the time we had attended all 356 of our showers, we could barely open the door to the room, and the bounty was piled about three feet high throughout the entire space. If one of our animals accidently entered the room, they were simply presumed dead, because it was unlikely they would navigate their way out any time soon.

Then, just before the baby arrived, we tackled the task of organizing the mass of stuff. We got huge flat plastic storage containers and sorted all the new and hand-me-down clothes by age and then piled them into the baby's little closet. After that we went about assembling and finding places for all the whatnots. There were chairs and swings and strollers and bouncers and highchairs and toys and blankets.

At the time we were living in a 1,200-square-foot house that wasn't exactly screaming out for more clutter. But clutter it we did. Every spare inch around the perimeter of the living room was jammed with a baby item. We tried to make it look nice, but the end result looked more like a garage sale than a living space. However, for the time being we could actually see the floor in the baby's room, and we appeared well equipped to tackle anything she threw at us.

Then the baby arrived.

At this point organization hit the fan in a spectacular fashion. Just like on *Hoarders*, our living space came to very accurately reflect our current mental state. As much as we tried (which, granted, wasn't that much in those first few weeks), we couldn't keep the house from looking like the Tasmanian Devil had wreaked havoc on a baby store (and also forgot to do the dishes). Then, just as we started to get a handle on the chaos, the child would wake up from her newborn slumber and actually start expressing interest in some of the nine hundred must-haves strewn around the house. In an effort to keep up with her attention span (or lack thereof), we made sure no happy baby aid was ever too far out of reach.

If I have to pinpoint it, I would have to say this is when the walls officially started coming in on all of us. Because literally, we started moving things from against the walls to the middle of the room. The poor animals had to navigate around toys on the floor, a swinging swing, and their owners threatening their lives if they made any noise at all while the baby was sleeping.

We immediately started dreaming of more square footage because we knew this problem was going to get much worse as time passed. For instance, the child currently weighed less than ten pounds and spent all her time propped up or lying wherever we chose to put her. And yet, she still monopolized every square foot of the house. I didn't want to imagine what was going to happen when she started moving of her own free will.

Turns out my suspicions were correct, and a mobile baby meant even more mess. Mostly because a mobile baby doesn't so much distinguish between baby must-haves and parent already-hads. The entire house became a playground for her exploring little mind and body. And who was I to argue when she found my DVD collection much more interesting than her blocks? I, too, would rather pull them off the shelf and open them one by one. I would also rather someone else cleaned up after me, if that could be arranged. So I could see why she found the activity so intriguing.

My overall strategy for maintaining my sanity during this time was to try to return all the clutter to its home at the end of the day. It was very, very tempting to just leave it out, because that's where it was all going to end up in twelve hours anyway, but I had to feel a small sense of victory over the chaos at least once a day, even if just for a brief moment.

The greatest part of all this was that even though quite a few of Vivian's whatnots were only must-haves for certain ages, we couldn't just discard or donate them after she aged out of them.

What if we had another baby at some point? We would need to use all this stuff again. So we had to find a way to store a mass of baby items for possible future use. Which, by the way, could be *years* from now. This is quite possibly the reason self-storage businesses were invented.

We didn't have the energy or inclination to explore any real storage options, so instead we just walked out to the converted garage, threw everything in there, and moved on. Ironically, the garage had been converted to a pub years prior, but you could now barely see the neon beer signs and dartboard peeking out from behind all the baby paraphernalia. It sorta looked like an abstract piece of art titled *Your Carefree Twenties Are Officially Over*. All I know for sure is if the *Hoarders* film crew wakes the baby when they arrive, I'm gonna be pissed.

This particular issue seemed to strike quite a chord with my MO-FLs. Lots of exclamation points in the responses to this one. It seems that no matter what your living situation, when you add a child and all the child's accessories (each sold separately), your home tends to shrink quite a bit. I would venture a guess that this has less to do with the actual physical space and more to do with the fact that your child's clutter taking over your home is the most unavoidable proof that everything has changed. Overall, it can be a bit jarring to have your personal space completely upended, especially in such a permanent manner.

Jill said she bought tubs to help with the organizing of kid stuff. "I also noticed how much crap my husband and I had. Lots of purging to make room for different crap." Nothing moves you into the next stage of your life quite like a hard shove from your due date rapidly approaching. "Don't hesitate, just purge! The babies are coming!"

A couple of the moms I talked to had moved into bigger homes prior to their child's arrival, only to find that there still wasn't enough room. This is because humans are like goldfish and tend to take up the exact amount of space we are allowed. When have you ever opened a cupboard in a home you've lived in for five years (or five months for that matter) and said, "Damn, totally empty. Sure wish I had some stuff to put in here." Never. That never happens. So it would follow that no matter what size home you move into, your little mini-goldfish will still manage to monopolize it. Babies are just that powerful.

Chipper Jen contributes her take. "Yesss!!! Crap everywhere! I had to buy lots of plastic containers and storage-type organizational items! Crazy how much stuff accumulates with tiny humans!" (Side note: Exclamation points are all the punctuation Chipper Jen needs in this life.)

Anna says that she and her husband are hoping to get out of their small house soon. "Our daughter has pretty much taken over every room. And yes, the storage has really been an issue. We plan to have another so I have kept everything—in the garage, attic, under beds, everyone's closet. A new house must happen before baby number two."

Sarah is working with her small space even as she adds another baby. "The poor new baby has to sleep in the dining room with the dog!" Having seen the size of Sarah's dog (a BIG Old English sheepdog), I'm a bit concerned about where exactly the baby is going to fit—unless he's going to sleep *on* the dog. Frankly that might be the biggest unclaimed space in the house.

For many, simply moving to a bigger house isn't a viable financial option, so they need to work with the space they have, or the space that their relatives have. Melanie says, "We have baby stuff everywhere. We have had to store items that we really like at my husband's parents' house until we can afford a bigger place."

On the other hand, like many of us, Melanie is constantly debating whether she should part with some of her loot. "I wish I could discipline myself to donate more items as Ian receives new, but I'm having difficulties parting with things."

And that's where the truth starts to rear its head, from beneath a pile of onesies and burp cloths. As much stuff as our kids bring into our lives, as much as they take our house and shake it up like a snow globe, the thought that we are done with the stuff—that they are done with the stuff—makes us a little sad. Sure, there will be another round of "stuff" for the next age, and the age after that, but we tend to hang on to that baby stuff a little longer than we probably should. This could mean a lot of things, but mostly it means that we haven't totally ruled out bringing home another baby to play with all this crap. Which in turn means we've made peace with the redecorating our first baby did to our house, and our life. Or maybe it means that we spent way too much money on all this stuff for it to be used only by one kid for fifteen minutes before he or she moved on to reorganizing our DVD collection. Could go either way.

Not too long ago my parents backed their truck up to my house and unloaded a stupid amount of boxes into my garage. My mother was absolutely giddy. The boxes, all labeled "Dawn," were full of remnants from my childhood: old stuffed animals, photo albums, favorite toys, dolls, recital costumes (So. Much. Fringe.), etc., etc. I was looking through all this stuff and thinking how special it was that my parents had kept it for me all these years. Then I remembered that I'm in my thirties and this crap had been taking up their space for three farkin' decades. I did not like what this meant for the future of my storage areas.

I looked up from my boxes to catch a glimpse of my parents gleefully pulling out of the driveway, light as feathers, returning home to their snow globe that was finally calm.

20

BABIES DON'T LIKE BRAGGING

(they can hear it, understand
it, and end it)

2:30 p.m.	vs.	2:30 a.m. (twelve hours later)
"He's doing great! Such a PERFECT baby!"		"If you go to sleep I promise I will never gloat again."

Parenting Rule #1

You are no longer in charge.

Parenting Rule #2

Never forget Rule #1.

Parenting Rule #3

If you forget Rule #1, it won't be long before you are reminded of Rule #1.

A t the beginning of your parenting adventure, your little ball of joy and love will constantly be throwing new challenges your way. First comes the "Living on Two Hours of Sleep at a Time" Challenge. Then the "Name the Most Surprising Place You've Found Poop on a Baby" Challenge. And a personal favorite, "How Do You Entertain a Baby While Your Boobs Are Being Sucked into a Breast Pump?" Challenge.

You will have a lot of ups and downs—a very bumpy road as you try to figure out this little person and how exactly you are going to manage to keep it and you alive long term. Eventually, though, you'll get into what feels like a groove. You may even think to yourself, *I GOT this*. I'm here to warn you, don't ever, ever say or even *think* the phrase "I GOT this." Ever.

You see, babies can't do much besides sleep, poop, and eat, but one of their highly unpublicized skills is their natural ability to sense when their parent is getting too comfortable. It is at that point that they will make sure the feeling doesn't last too long. All of a sudden that magic swing you were raving about in your moms group doesn't lull her to sleep, he starts spitting up again after feeding, or she'll become completely inconsolable for two hours in the middle of the night, after having slept through the night for weeks.

Some may say this is just growing pains. I say it is your baby making sure there is no bragging going on anywhere, even if it's only in your own head.

Whenever someone would ask about how Vivian was doing, we would give the standard "Really great!" answer. Occasionally my partner would boast, "She slept through the night last night!" At which point I would slap her on the arm and tell her to shut her mouth. Because, without fail, every single damn time we would boast or go on about how perfect our child was, everything would go to crap the very next day. Then I would scream, "Why did you say she was perfect???"

It got to the point, and we continue this today, where our answer would be, "She's okay. She could be better." It's not the nicest thing to say about your child, but for the sake of self-preservation, we downplay her accomplishments like crazy. We never want her to catch wind of us bragging and feel the need to remind us who decides how things are going to play out around here.

21

YOU CAN'T AFFORD THIS

(adorableness does not come cheap)

The ways children waste money:

- They need a new wardrobe every three months.

- They throw half their restaurant meal on the floor.

- It costs 25¢ in wipes every time they go to the bathroom.

- They need educational toys, but then as they get smarter they need new educational toys. A vicious, costly cycle.

- Too many educational toys may lead to college, which is very expensive. Proceed with caution.

Mantras of the frugal parent:

- "Wearing only hand-me-down clothes is good for the environment."

- "Who needs toys when nature has provided rocks and dirt aplenty?"

- "You know, a lot of really successful people didn't even go to college."

I recently read that it costs about $300,000 to raise a child, and that's not counting college tuition. My kid is not even two years old, and I feel as if she's already cost at least $150,000—with $135,000 having gone to baby supply stores and the other $15,000 to fresh fruit that went bad thirteen minutes after having been purchased.

The long and the short of it is: you can't afford this child. Remember all those fancy meals out (and by fancy, I mean meals out), vacations, and clothes you used to buy? All that money is now going toward adorable whatnots that will be used by your child for approximately three days before they (1) grow out of it, (2) grow tired of it, or (3) eat it.

Baby stores are by far the biggest money suck that exists for parents. They remind me a lot of Target, in that I go in for one $10 item and can't get out without spending at least $287. They are evil like that. Sometimes I even forego a shopping cart in these stores, thinking that without a carrying device I simply won't have the ability to amass a large bounty of goods. During those trips I inevitably end up in the checkout line barely able to see over the pile of merchandise I have precariously balanced in my arms, my child buried underneath the necessities I've loaded on her stroller.

The internet is also a large recipient of my spontaneous baby spending. It is deep and alluring and offers me click after recommended click of wonderful must-haves to peruse and purchase. Before I know it, two to five days later, a steady stream of boxes starts showing up at my door, each one a small piece of evidence that I have no self-control whatsoever. Many times, since my memory is shot to hell (see Chapter 26, "Remember Your Memory?"), the contents are as much a surprise to me as they are to the rest of the household. Sure, it can get expensive, but it's sorta like Christmas morning with all of us gathered around opening up my boxes of unneeded internet purchases.

Please keep in mind that I've made all these purchases on top of the roughly $4 million worth of hand-me-downs we were given by generous parents who wanted their spontaneous purchases to live on with another child. Every time Vivian reaches a new size of clothes, I go into her closet and pull out another bin of hand-me-downs. These are perfectly good clothes purchased by parents who most likely weren't thinking of my closet when they forked over their cash. And yet, even with all that generosity, I'm still going broke with baby purchases.

As soon as we got pregnant with baby number two, I did the math and realized that we would save roughly $13 million if the next child were also a girl. Of course, I had the ultrasound and it's a boy, so now I'm grappling with the fact that I have effectively spent thousands of dollars on clothes that were sometimes used only a few times before being tossed into the hand-me-down pile. Off to live on at another home, while we start over with a new gender.

One of the sneakiest and most costly parts of raising a kid is the fact that, in addition to clothing them and providing them with toys, you also have to feed them. I know, the hits just keep on coming, don't they? If you choose not to breastfeed, or aren't able to, you will feel the financial burden of feeding your baby early on. Formula does not come cheap. I'm thinking this might have something to do with it being pretty much your only option for feeding your newborn if a boob isn't available. They have you backed into a bit of a corner.

I was able to primarily breastfeed for the first ten months, with some formula supplementing in later months. I remember being so eager for the baby to get older and start eating real food. Then she got older and I realized I was responsible for buying her that real food. This put a damper on my excitement. Instead of simply whipping out my boob, I had to whip up food. And unlike my boob, there was quite a variety of solid food I could offer her. She started out with baby food, so I would buy an entire aisle worth of pureed goodness. Then, as she moved on to more substantial food, I would buy out the baby snacks aisle. Eventually she arrived at real food (as much real food as can be eaten by someone with four teeth). I wanted to make sure I didn't skimp on nutrition, so I bought organic this and fresh that. Three days later everything would go bad, and I would have to head back to the store for more healthy goodness. It still seems as if I go to the store at least four times a week to get food for this child, and she weighs only twenty-two pounds. I don't like where this is heading for my bank account.

And it doesn't stop at food and clothes. If you are a working parent, you need to plan to spend more than your monthly mortgage on daycare. If you care about your child's physical and mental development, there are gymnastics classes, art classes, and swimming lessons. You are a horrible parent if you don't do all these things and take 34,533 photos of every moment.

And then, if you're lucky and you've done a good job with this child, guess what your reward is? You get to pay for four to eight years of college!! Long story short: You aren't going on another vacation for the next twenty-five years. But you can spend your spare time making an elaborate kickass quilt out of onesies your kid wore twice, and that sounds like just as much fun, really.

I asked my MOFLs for advice about avoiding bankruptcy before your child is five years old. Turns out my moms are a thrifty bunch and had some good tips.

Chipper Jen does not recommend big box baby stores for saving money. "Baby stores are great for first-time parents who are having a shower. People (i.e., grandparents, new aunts, kidless best friends, etc.) LOVE to spend money on new babies for showers. It's appealing as a one-stop shop with lots of options. But not for everyday purchases." Instead, Jen bargain-shops at consignment stores or the discount rack at Target and Marshalls.

Viki recommends steering clear of department stores. "Garage sales are great. I'm a mom who won't break the bank for a kid who grows so fast."

Brooke discovered a fun event. "Just Between Friends Sales (www.jbfsale.com) happen twice a year, and you can buy everything you need for all ages/sizes. It's awesome and the prices are garage-sale prices!"

Salpy has some tried-and-true advice from experience. "Read *Baby Bargains*. A great book with great ideas. I'd say wait to see if you really need something. Borrow, look at online marketplaces, and go to garage sales and consignment stores as much as possible for clothes and big things. Don't skimp on car seats, though!"

Amy, mom of three boys, points out the positive of her situation. "Only produce one gender of children and save all their stuff. It's working for me."

In addition to the above, my general advice is to stay far, far away from big box baby stores. They have a way of pulling you in even if you are only in the general vicinity. Also, cancel your internet and cell phone until your child is fifteen years old. That is the only way to ensure you won't fall victim to a late-night buying binge. It's embarrassing when your family finds you the next morning, laptop or phone fallen to your side, fourteen browser windows open, and credit cards strewn all about. All they can do is look wearily to the front door and wait for the impending barrage of deliveries to arrive.

PARTNER CORNER: ALL THE THINGS

Pat: Luckily, we had friends that gave us a lot of stuff before we had our baby. So, once you know you are going to have a baby, reach out to everyone with young kids and ask for hand-me-downs. Most people will let you have old stuff, or at least borrow until they have more kids. Sound machines are necessary, so get ten.

Larry: Oh, my! We wasted so much money on the latest and greatest. It wasn't until the second child that we caught on to the fact that hand-me-downs were just perfect for a being that changes shape and size monthly. As far as must-haves go, we would have paid double for a good baby carrier/wrap. We wouldn't have made it without those.

22

TEETH ARE THE DEVIL

(and your child is possessed)

The evolution of teeth

Toothless happy newborn

▼

Tooth by excruciating tooth pierces through innocent baby's gums

▼

Tooth-filled happy child

▼

Tooth by tooth falls or is forcibly pulled out of child's head

▼

Permanent teeth emerge

▼

Painful years of braces

▼

Cavities, oral surgery, gum disease

▼

Toothless happy senior

have some bad news for you. You may want to sit down for it; it's not pretty.

You will spend the first few months of your child's life getting settled in, battling sleep deprivation and explosive diarrhea, and wondering when it will all start to get easier. And then, because God loves you, or perhaps due to a biological mechanism that's meant to keep the species alive, things do get a little easier. Or maybe you are just getting used to it being hard? Either way, you aren't as overwhelmed. Life feels like it could maybe even be normal again someday soon.

And then. And then. And then. Juuuuuust as you are getting ready to proclaim your mastery of this parenting gig, out of nowhere, solid objects start forcing their way through your child's face.

Teeth, while I can see their general overall purpose, are the devil. Plain and simple. It is absolutely unnatural (and yet, I'm assuming actually pretty natural) the way they take root in your kid's face, push their way out slowly but painfully, and then eventually bust through the skin and into the world. It's like a horror movie where the victim is just sitting there while random sharp objects burst through his face.

But this isn't a horror movie; this is your life. Mother Nature is the director of your life, and she has a unique schedule in mind for your child's teeth. The schedule goes something like this: "Is everything going well in this household? Yes? Okay, let's rip some faces apart."

Out of nowhere this baby that you naively thought you had a handle on will turn into a blood-curdling banshee. And there is nothing you can really do to stop it.

Teeth do most of their damage to your life *before* you ever get a chance to actually see them. As they grow out of wherever they are growing and slowly make their way up into the world, they are causing your little one a great deal of pain. This becomes a ton of fun for you because your little one doesn't quite have a handle on communication beyond screaming his or her head off. The child is unable to say something helpful like, "Mommy, my face hurts like hell." All they can do is scream at the top of their lungs. Conveniently, this is also their selected form of communication to let you know when they are hungry, tired, wet, cold, hot, or in the mood to scream at the top of their lungs.

Over time you will come to know the telltale signs your child gives when confronted with a new tooth, but in the beginning you are left guessing as to what is really going on. The good news is, even when you figure out what is going on, there still isn't much you can do about it. You just have to sit back and watch as the devil teeth make their way through your child's gums one at an excruciating time.

Another great thing about teeth? You have no idea when they will decide to make their appearance. After Vivian got her first tooth, we waited so long for the second one I started to think maybe baby dentures were in her future. If only we had been so lucky. But no, one at a time, whenever the universe felt like we were getting too much sleep, an evil tooth would appear. She still doesn't have all her teeth, and I feel like we've been going through this for the past two decades. Seriously, how many farkin' teeth does one child need? Aren't they all going to fall out eventually anyway? Why are we wasting so much time on these first ones?

Someone needs to invent a drug that brings all teeth in at the same time. It would be a hellish week or two, but at the end, BAM, all the teething would be taken care of, and chewing would commence immediately! Right after a long celebratory nap.

For our kid, the toughest time she has when she's teething is at night. This works out really well because that is when I have the easiest time sleeping. Our once-peaceful sleeper wakes up several times a night screaming in pain. In the beginning I frantically Googled "teething remedies" and didn't find much that worked, or that I was willing to try. She thought her frozen teething rings or rags were toys, and they usually ended up being chewed on by the dogs after she quickly lost interest in them. There were topical numbing gels, but something about putting a random gel in my baby's mouth didn't seem right. Plus, I somehow doubted that they would keep her numb for the entire eight hours I was wanting to sleep. I also read about teething tablets, but unfortunately they had been recalled for reasons that scared me off any other product, natural or otherwise.

On a side note, my single favorite internet community board post ever was one written by a very pleased mother who was posting about recalled teething tablets. "I'm so glad I stocked up on teething tablets before they were recalled!! You can't find them anywhere now!!" Posts like this make me feel so much better about Vivian's overall chances with us as her parents. I may print it out and show it to her someday. "See! You could have people like this for parents, so stop complaining."

When she was old enough, and after it was okayed by our pediatrician, we started giving her a little bit of baby Tylenol or ibuprofen. I'm not sure how effective these were because I was too freaked out to give her the recommended portion, and usually gave her only about half of what she was supposed to get. That was probably just enough to make her realize she really wanted more.

Ultimately, although it was against our nighttime rules, a lot of times we would pick the baby up and just hold her in the rocking chair until she calmed down. That calm usually lasted until the time we put her back in her crib. Which made for nonstop excitement all night long.

I have very little advice for you with regards to dealing with teething, other to warn you again that teeth are the devil. They seem to be another one of your great parenting hurdles that no one feels the need to tell you about before you bring the baby home. Maybe they think ignorance is bliss, and the less you know about your impending struggles the better? Perhaps. But ignorance becomes decidedly less blissful when woken from a peaceful slumber by an inconsolable infant. And even more so when it happens seven times a night.

The good news is (you've been waiting for good news, right?) there is a chance your kid won't have any reaction to his or her face being torn apart by teeth. I know this because I've had some friends say things like, "Yeah, we went to the doctor and found out that the baby had all sorts of teeth! Crazy, we didn't even know they came in!" I hate these friends and don't like talking to them very much at all.

I asked my MOFLs about their experiences with devil teeth and found that most of them agreed with my description. It is not a coincidence teeth are shaped like horns, let me tell you.

Carrie says, "I agree that teeth are the devil, or at least they are when they are coming in. My first has the hardest time. He is a horrible sleeper and eater, moody, cranky, and the list goes on and on whenever he is teething. I thought we were done with all that, and then here come the two-year molars. I'm convinced it will never end."

Dana agrees. "I have no tips or tricks for dealing. It just sucks all the way around. Seriously any time my child was sad, mad, a bad sleeper, bad napper, bad eater, it was always because she was getting a tooth. My only tip is to not get too down on yourself when this happens. It's hard because you can't do much to help them. Most babies just want their mom, so just give lots of hugs and cuddles."

Michelle recommends helping the baby with medication. "Don't be afraid to give Advil or Tylenol for the pain. It will help everyone sleep better and is recommended by my pediatrician over topical numbing agents. If my teeth hurt, I take something for the pain, so why should I make my baby suffer when it helps?"

And then there are people like Sarah, whom we have agreed we hate, because her kids didn't have bad teething experiences. "For my kids it's never been too big of a deal, other than biting while nursing."

Somehow I am a little satisfied that at least Sarah had to deal with her babies chomping on her nipples, so that she knows some of the pain the rest of us go through with teething. She did offer this solution for the chomping, though: "A family friend told me to flick their face. I did. They stopped."

If only that advice could work for all of our troubles with babies . . .

23

YOU'LL BE BLAMED IN THERAPY SOMEDAY

(in case you were wondering
if the fun ever stops)

The bad news:

Your child will grow up to have lots of issues.

The good news:

People without issues are boring.

H ere's the thing. You're going to mess this parenting thing up. The sooner you accept it, the sooner you can stop being so worried about messing this parenting thing up. Now, I'm not talking about the FBI investigation type of messing up, because you should still be aiming to keep mug shots out of the baby book. The messing up I'm speaking of is the "So, Mom, I've been seeing a therapist and she suggested maybe you come in for a session" type. Oh yes, that will happen.

I pride myself on being surrounded by a diversity of people, from a diversity of backgrounds. And it turns out I'm a pretty good listener. These facts combine to give me unique insight into a lot of different kinds of people. And guess what? We're all messed up. In some way, we all have "stuff." We all have baggage and issues and insecurities and fears. No matter where we came from or how we were raised. So, just playing the odds here, all our kids are going to have "stuff," too. It's unavoidable.

Sometimes I get my stomach in knots thinking about the kind of life I want my kid to have: the things I want to protect her from, the opportunities I want to present to her, the unconditional love and support I want to offer her from now until forever. And then I realize, no matter what I do or how well I do it, she's still going to grow up with issues. And those issues will be my doing—at least most of them will. (I'm sure adolescent heartache will be responsible for some as well.)

You can spin yourself around in circles trying to make the right choices for your kid, hoping that somehow you will stumble upon the formula for creating a perfectly well-adjusted adult. Every option (breastfeed / don't breastfeed, daycare / stay at home, cry it out / attachment) has two (or more) sides to it. And if you're crazy like me, then all it takes is thirty seconds in your brain for every one of those sides to lead to a horrible childhood and an unstable adulthood. I mean, we are responsible for a real live PERSON here, people. This is not to be taken lightly.

But then I realize: I love my kid and I want the best things for her. I look out for her interests above my own and give her as many kisses as she will allow. And you know what? That might be enough. At the very least it's not a bad place to start.

Here's my way of trying to make myself feel better when I start to worry that I will be an utter parental failure. I tell myself, "Self, I'm thinking that the people who are *actually* failing at parenting probably don't spend any time at all wondering if they are good parents. Much like crazy people have no idea they are crazy." So, basically, if you are constantly wondering whether you are a good parent, then you probably aren't half bad. Crap moms have far too many other things on their minds to be spending time worrying about kids.

And let's be honest, issues aren't always a bad thing, so maybe it's not the end of the world if your kid picks up a few along the way. Issues make people who they are, and they can challenge people to want to be better. And frankly, adults without some decent issues are just plain boring, if you ask me.

Sometimes I look around at my kid's spoiled little life and wonder where her struggles will come from—because she's got a pretty easy road ahead of her. Struggle builds character, wanting builds grit—so where will Vivi find those things?

Luckily for me, Vivian has two moms, which is probably going to be a struggle for her at some point. I really doubt, given our community, friends, and family, that this is going to be a *huge* struggle, but I can hope.

The most important thing to remember is this: Something you do or don't do or think about doing but don't do or do too much will inevitably lead to your child having issues when they are older. No matter what you do, this will happen, so go ahead and forgive yourself for it now, and stop taking everything so damn seriously.

And don't worry; in thirty short years your kid may have a baby of his or her own. And when that great day arrives, you will be vindicated. Finally something will click in your child's head, and they will realize what you went through in trying to corral them through their childhood. All of a sudden the lack of mug shots (yours or theirs) in the baby book will seem like a monumental accomplishment.

24

YOU CAN'T HAVE IT ALL

(unless you plan on sucking at most of it)

Before baby **daily to-do list**	vs.	**After baby** **daily to-do list**
Morning jog		Try to make sure everyone in the house is fed and bathed on a semiregular basis
Client conference call		
Kick the crap out of my email inbox		
Lunch with colleagues		
Oil change		
Finish three projects; start four more		
Drinks with friends		
Gourmet cooking class		
Catch up on DVR shows		
Read a four-hundred-page novel		

We are an interesting generation of women, those of us raising kids in the modern era. Most of our mothers were raised by stay-at-home moms, during a time when pretty much all moms were stay-at-home moms. Our mothers were either a part of or just after the women's liberation movement, when women marched into the workplace with their heads held high. A lot of our moms worked because they really wanted to, because their family couldn't survive on one income, or a combo of the two. We grew up with media images of strong working moms all over the place.

Our generation, or at least my circle of friends, seems to be in a bit of a conundrum compared to those who came before us. We are waiting later and later to have kids, which means most of us have an established career going by the time our babies come along. This leaves moms with a very real and difficult choice: stay in the workforce and arrange for childcare, or put their career on hold to stay home with their child until they are school age or older.

It's not an easy choice to make, especially for those who have spent years in school and on the job working their butts off to get to a certain level professionally. We take pride in our work, and we enjoy what we do. But we were also hoping to be good moms as well. Is it possible to do everything?

Because I was an avid TV viewer before I had a child, I knew that it was very possible to have a successful career, wonderful relationship, funny children, and a size 6 waistline all at the same time. This much I knew for sure. If Rachel on *Friends*, and Miranda on *Sex and the City*, and those doctors on *Grey's Anatomy* taught me anything, it's that kids have very little impact on your life and career. So I just knew I was going to be a-okay.

But it turns out all those bitches were lying. And also perhaps made-up characters that don't actually exist in real life. Both of these facts are extremely disappointing.

In reality it is very, very hard to juggle everything required to "have it all." And most of the time you feel like at least one or two balls are constantly hitting the floor because there's no way to keep them all up in the air.

I have a unique situation in that I work for myself, from home. One might think this is the perfect situation for a new mom—a great way to be home with the baby and earn money! However, one would be very misguided in that thought. The absolute worst part about working for yourself is that there is no such thing as maternity leave for the self-employed. Sure, you can take time off, and you can even collect disability if you arrange it right. But clients tend to have needs no matter what your sleep-deprivation level is. And if you are interested in still having those clients after your maternity leave, it's highly recommended that you not force them to use someone else to provide your service.

In my case, after a few days off while I was in the hospital, I got back to work immediately. Now, I'm not talking eight-hour days; I was just doing small projects here and there. My partner, on the other hand, is a CPA with many a tax client. Our child was born in the middle of March. The tax deadline is April 15. Needless to say, our first month or so home with the baby wasn't exactly the peaceful bonding experience we were dreaming of when planning a family.

And honestly it's felt like a bit of a cluster ever since. We have a babysitter at least three days a week for about six hours at a time, but before the baby came along I was working at least forty hours a week. This means I now do a lot of working during naptimes and after bedtime. Every once in a while I consider putting her in daycare, but then when it's time to pull the trigger I just can't do it. I'm not sure why exactly. After all, I was in daycare from six months on, and I don't remember anything traumatizing about the experience. In fact, I think daycare would go a long way in helping to socialize my shy little girl. And educationally they would probably focus on a lot of things I just don't get around to. But I still can't do it.

I've realized recently that this hesitation is about me, not my kid. It's not that I think daycare is bad; it's that I think I'll regret not spending more time with her while she was young. That I will look back and wish that I had juggled a little better to make being with her a bigger priority.

I'm in a unique in-between position where I am able to work and keep my kid at home. I don't have the definite "I'm going to work, and she must go to daycare" or the "I'm staying home with the kids instead of going to work." So I end up just spinning around trying to figure out what the best answer is for all of us, even though I doubt there is just one right answer.

I still hold on to the notion that I can somehow do everything. I can continue my career that I've worked so hard to build, I can be there for my child the way I always dreamed I would be, I can be a good partner by nurturing our relationship, and I can remain fulfilled with activities outside the home. But when I actually try to do everything, I always end up feeling as if I'm just doing everything really poorly. My work doesn't get done as quickly as it should, and sometimes not as well as it should. My kid spends too much time watching TV when I should be playing with her or otherwise engaging her in brain-growing activities. My partner and I rarely get around to date nights because we are just too damned tired to even plan one. And my precious alone time, when I'm able to refuel on quiet and solitude, is a long-distant memory.

But then I have to remind myself every day how incredibly blessed I am to have the life I have. That I'm able to rearrange things a little bit and spend most of my days with my child. That she has both of her parents there when she wakes up and when she goes to sleep. That I have an amazing support system to pick up the slack when I can't do it all, and they are all people Vivian adores.

In the end I've realized that my child will be fine whether or not she is in daycare. I know because I am fine, and I never felt neglected at all by the fact that my parents both had full-time jobs. I think the biggest lesson I was taught by my parents, the one that has made the most positive impact on who I am today, is that you need to always show up for the things that really matter. My mom never missed a silly school event, even though it must have meant crazy juggling at work. ("Sure, honey, I can be at your 10:00 a.m. pancake breakfast that fits ever so nicely into my schedule and totally doesn't add two hours of commuting to my day.") Both of my parents were always at all of my roughly five million sporting events over the years, no matter how bad my team was. I always had a ride to the countless extracurricular activities I signed up for. They were always home for dinner. And they always fought fiercely to make sure I got the best education possible. In short, they showed up.

I know my parents had struggles over the years and definitely made sacrifices of their own dreams so that mine had a greater chance of success. But somehow they pulled it all off, and somehow I'll pull it off as well, even if sometimes it feels as if I'm barely hanging on to any of it at all.

The only real advice I have for you in this area of sucking at all the things is that you should try to make it a priority to keep doing all the things. It will be very easy to let things like date night and alone time and one-on-one time with your kid slip by the wayside. Things get to be very overwhelming, your days get to be very short, and sometimes you instinctively go into survival mode. A mode in which the minimum gets done just to keep your head above water, or, in this case, your head above insanity.

It will seem hard, but force yourself to regularly arrange a day, or at least an afternoon, alone. Make an agreement with your partner that you each get to participate in an activity outside of the family, and cover for each other to make that possible. Make date night a regularly scheduled event, even if it's just a quick dinner down at the greasy spoon. Let the dishes go for one night, and get down on the floor and wrestle with your kid, absorbing all that silly laughter. In short, always show up for the things that matter, and make sure that you are one of those things.

My MOFLs are a diverse set of moms, with the number of stay-at-home moms about equal to the number of working moms. I asked the moms who work how they deal with everything and whether they regret not spending more time with their kids. I asked the stay-at-home moms why they decided to stay home and if they regret missing out on a career. What I got was a nice mix of answers that show there are a lot of ways of looking at these issues.

Sarah was the most adamant among the working moms about wanting to work. This might have something to do with the fact that she went to college for over nine years to become a veterinarian and had been working professionally for only three and a half years when she had her first child. Obviously she was committed to her profession and enjoyed it, so it was a big priority for her to keep working. I think this is the case for many moms: their work isn't just a way to make money—it is a part of who they are.

Sarah says, "I am a woman who was NOT meant to stay home. My kids are my life and maternity leave is awesome, but I love what I do and I love adult contact! I did struggle with guilt when I went back after my first son, but it quickly went away. I'm lucky that I have my parents and my best friend watching my kids. And I work four ten-hour days, so I get three days a week with them. I wouldn't be happy or fulfilled without work. I think/hope I will be a better mom because I work."

Dana was still on maternity leave when she answered my question. "I feel like my answer is going to be different now than it will be in six weeks when I have to go back to work. Right now I don't want to go back. I really wish I could stay home while my kids are young and go back once they are in school full time, but that just doesn't make sense financially if we ever want to retire, send our kids to college, or go on a vacation. We like the lifestyle both incomes afford us, and things would be a lot different on one income. On the other hand, after I went back last time and got into the swing of things, I was happy to be there and have adult time, adult conversations, and to be able to run errands on my lunch break ALONE. I also really love my childcare provider, and I would seriously be sad if she weren't in my kids' lives on a regular basis."

Moving over to the stay-at-home mom category, Amy made that choice a long time ago. "I always planned on being a stay-at-home mom, so my husband and I prepared for it from day one, before we were even married. It affected every choice we made, from cars we purchased, to homes we bought. I absolutely plan to go back to work full time when the kids are older. I am staying home because I want to care for them, not because I didn't enjoy working. I do not care if my career suffers. I'm sure that it has and will continue to do so. Working is great and I enjoyed many aspects of my jobs in the past, but a family is the only thing in life I ever KNEW for a FACT I wanted. I think my kids are fabulous, and I'm honored to be the one who gets to spread peanut butter and jelly on their bread. No really, I'm actually serious. And when I have too much going on, too many commitments to keep, I absolutely feel like I'm sucking at everything. So for now I try to make sure I'm not sucking at the things that are most important to me."

Sommer has a somewhat unique struggle. She had to give up her career that she really enjoyed when she got married because her husband's career moved the family around quite a bit. This meant she could never take a job of her own without the fear that she would have to quit abruptly.

"This has been a very, VERY difficult struggle for me. Because of my husband's career, it's impossible to have my own. We don't know where we will be living from one year to the next. Basically, my ambitions/goals are put on hold for my husband and my son. I feel blessed that I'm provided for and am able to be with my baby boy. But it also leaves me guessing about who I am as an individual. I love my sweet baby boy and my amazing husband, and for now my purpose in life is to be the supporter and run the show behind the scenes, but sometimes I feel unfulfilled as my own woman. And sometimes I'm scared that I'll lose a part of myself and my dreams with being consumed with my family. It's hard to learn the balance between mother, wife, and individual. And, I think all roles are super-important for happiness. It's a juggling act."

Sommer touches on what we all are going through, to a certain extent, trying to figure out a way to maintain ourselves and the things that made us ourselves before our kids came along. Especially when it's so easy to let those things slip away as they are replaced with the new parts of ourselves brought along by the kids. It's hard to find a way for everything to be maintained without being left feeling as if parts are lacking.

This issue goes much deeper than just the work/stay-at-home debate; it really goes back to those damn TV shows we've watched over the years. We would watch Clair Huxtable or Elyse Keaton and think, *Look how happy and pretty they are! I will grow up to be just like them!* We've had these images in our heads for years, of how our life would be, or how we would be. And sometimes when we look in the mirror or around at our house or buckle our kids in for our early-morning routine, we stop and think, *Clair Huxtable was much better at this and always looked so good, too!*

But hey, parenting, if you are doing it right, is hard. Be gentle with yourself; realize Clair and Elyse had great hair and makeup people, thirty minutes to solve all their parenting problems, and weren't real people. Stop holding yourself up to an image you created before you were actually part of it. Forgive yourself from the very beginning for not being as crafty or as organized or as perfect as you always envisioned you would be. Look in your baby's little eyes and realize that, to them, you are just about as perfect as they come.

25

A DYSFUNCTIONAL RELATIONSHIP

(there will be tears)

Parenting highs	vs.	Parenting lows
Smiles!		No sleeping!
Sleep through the night!		Teeth = Screaming through the night!
Playdates!		Viruses!
Crawling!		Bumps and bruises!
Solid foods!		Picky eater = Throws solid foods on the ground!
Personality!		Stubbornness!
Smooth sailing!		More f'n teeth!!!!

H ave you ever had this conversation with a friend over appetizers and drinks?

"Are things going better with you and Person You're Dating?"

"You know, we had a really good couple weeks, and then it all
went to crap again. I don't know what the problem is. I think Person
I'm Dating is so great, but then sometimes they treat me so poorly.
Just when I think I can't take anymore, Person I'm Dating becomes
a sweetheart again, showers me with love and affection, and things
are wonderful. Until they aren't. It'll probably work out though,
right? Because when it's good, it is really, really good."

At this point you are usually shoveling appetizers into your
mouth with abandon, trying to avoid telling this friend that they
are in an extremely dysfunctional relationship. Because, let's be
honest, if they haven't figured it out themselves, then you're probably not going to convince them over bruschetta. This friend needs
a shrink, and you need to get through the meal without having to
destroy their delusions.

Dysfunctional relationships are marked by a very real cycle of
Horrible Awful Times, followed by Ecstatically Blissful Times. Repeat. Forever. Luckily for you, parenting also adheres to this very
healthy cycle.

Recently, I had this conversation:

"How's the baby?"

"Oh, she's great this week. Last week she was hell on wheels. She
was up all night screaming her face off because she had a cold AND
two teeth coming in. She couldn't breathe, her face was exploding
with teeth, and she was miserable. No sleep for anyone. This week
the cold cleared up, and the teeth popped through, and we are all so
happy you'd think we were mainlining Disney fairy dust."

"How many more teeth still have to come in?"

"I don't want to talk about it. Let me stay on the fairy dust for a while please."

Welcome to the wonderful cycle called parenting. Even if you managed to avoid them your whole life, you are now stuck in a long-term dysfunctional relationship. And there is no therapist who can, through their sage advice and sympathetic nod, help you figure out a way to extricate yourself from your situation. (There are, however, fantastic sales on wine pretty much every day. Coincidence?)

So what are you to do?

I say embrace it. I say act exactly like you are in a dysfunctional relationship. Stay with me here. When things are going great in un-stable relationships, one or both parties always has a naive belief that things have actually changed, that everything is wonderful, and that all their problems have been solved. The bliss is high and the denial higher, because they don't actually acknowledge that they are on a never-ending merry-go-round of dysfunction. You, however, are going to own it.

When everything is going fine with your kid (no snot, lots of sleep, giggles aplenty), grab onto those moments and store them in your heart and mind under "Good Times." Take note of them; jot them down in your diary with smiley faces next to them. Collect photos and videos to document them. Do not take them for granted. Do not quickly move about your day because you are so happy that your kid is letting you quickly move about your day. And most important, DO NOT for one second naively believe that you have this parenting thing figured out and are ready to be featured on the covers of advice magazines. (Please see Chapter 20, "Babies Don't Like Bragging.")

When the baby is being an angel, get down on the floor with them or pick them up, or just stop for five minutes and absorb this brief moment of calm. Bury your face in your child's neck and tell them you love them so, so much. Breathe in their beautiful only-from-a-baby smell. Tell yourself you are so, so lucky. Do all this with the very real knowledge that this moment is only temporary and that this bliss will not last (in fact, sometimes it won't even last the five minutes you are on the floor).

Eventually something will happen to shift the tides; it always does. A tooth will rip its way through your child's head and result in forty-eight hours of blood-curdling screaming. (Please see Chapter 22, "Teeth Are the Devil.") A butterfly will sneeze on the baby and she will catch the All Snot, All the Time Virus that makes breathing, sleeping, and eating nearly impossible tasks. Or maybe nothing weird will happen at all, but the kid will still decide on a whim that rolling around on the ground screaming is their preferred form of communication.

These less-than-blissful periods of time will feel absolutely endless, because nothing makes time slow waaaaay down quite like lack of sleep combined with a screaming baby. In fact, let's simplify it: Nothing makes time slow down like lack of sleep. Done. Period. Time stopped. And even though it's not logical, you will start to convince yourself that the rest of your life will be spent in this state of sleep deprivation and tantrums. Clearly you've broken the baby and there is no fix in sight.

This is where the understanding of your dysfunctional relationship comes in. Put your head down, weather this storm, and realize that it will only be a matter of time before your baby is bringing you flowers to apologize for screaming at you endlessly the other night. He might even throw in some high-fives to really win you back.

Always, always, always remember this: Your relationship with this child is a cyclical one that never stops cycling until hopefully he or she finally moves out of your house (after moving back in three times) when they are twenty-five (or thirty-five) years old. Also, never, ever, ever naively believe that the good times will last indefinitely. This will help you avoid the Bad Times Whiplash that can occur when teeth or a flu bug or the teenage years hit out of nowhere.

Amy, one of my MOFLs, said it best: "I was always anxious that a difficult phase would never pass: I would never sleep again, never eat a meal in peace again, never get to shave my legs again. But my motto became 'This too shall pass.' Nothing with your baby is permanent. Enjoy when they are lovely, and don't freak out when they are difficult for days on end, because neither phase lasts."

Also, go ahead and take advantage of those wine sales when they are happening. Never a bad idea to stock up in preparation for the next bad times storm front.

26

REMEMBER YOUR MEMORY?

(it had a good run)

YOUR BRAIN PRE-BABY	vs.	YOUR BRAIN POST-BABY
Razor-sharp		Similar to that "This is your brain on drugs" commercial, only without the fun of being high on drugs first
Capable of storing mental notes		
Able to hold onto a thought for longer than 1.3 seconds		Responsible for lots of blank stares

EVOLUTION OF AN IMPORTANT THOUGHT PRE-BABY	vs.	EVOLUTION OF AN IMPORTANT THOUGHT POST-BABY
1. Have a thought		1. Have a thought
2. Remember the thought		2. Stand up immediately and look for your phone or a piece of paper on which to record the thought
3. The end		3. Go into the other room, trying desperately to remember the thought while you continue your search
		4. See a shiny object
		5. Forget the thought
		6. Stand in the middle of the new room, trying to remember the thought
		7. Go back to previous room, hoping something will trigger the thought back
		8. Three days later, have the thought again
		9. Repeat from #1

One of the more alarming side effects of bringing home a baby is that apparently you are required to leave your memory at the hospital in exchange for your new child. It's best that you prepare for this now. How do you prepare? Stock up on Post-It Notes, get to know the Notes app in your phone, and alert your friends and family members that you are about to become very, very stupid.

I'm not sure what exactly causes our memories to crap out when we have a baby, but I would venture a guess that it is a combination of New Parenthood's Greatest Hits (sleep deprivation, hormones gone whack-a-doodle, and way too much new information flooding in all at once). All these add together to make your brain a useless blob of flesh that can leave you standing in the grocery store with one item in your cart trying to remember why you came there in the first place.

Important dates and conversation details will flee your brain instantly. Finding an object by implementing the "retrace your steps" strategy will leave you about 61,346 steps shy of recovering the item. ("Well, I know I got out of bed this morning, but beyond that I don't have any concrete details.")

The most alarming loss for me, as a writer and previously somewhat intelligent human, was the absolute annihilation of my vocabulary. All of a sudden the simplest words disappeared from my brain. The other day I literally spent five minutes doing an elaborate charades spectacle in the middle of a conversation while trying to get to the word "rug." Rug. That's three letters and—poof—it was just gone from my brain.

Often I will be talking to someone and up ahead in my thought I can see a huge hole where a word should be. I will try to slow down and give my brain time to come up with the word or perhaps think of an alternative. But more times than not I will just start snapping my fingers and shaking my head, hoping that combination will somehow summon the word forth to my lips. This is particularly fun in professional situations.

In all seriousness, I found my memory loss and general stupidity not only inconvenient but quite alarming as well. I was used to being on top of things, successfully managing multiple projects at once and using words bigger than two syllables. Then all of a sudden my brain just went sloooow. My quick wit would limp into a conversation half-heartedly; my confidence took a hit when it came to speaking and writing, two things that used to come easily. This was all such a nice addition to the other less-than-stellar feelings I was having about myself where this parenting adventure was concerned.

My child is about eighteen months old as I write this book, and I will say that I feel a little more on the ball these days than I have previously. I'm honestly not sure if that means that my brain recovered or if I've simply gotten better at dealing with my deficiencies. I never leave the house without a list of some sort. If I have a thought, I act on it instantly, or at least write it down right away. And I've gotten a lot better at simply navigating around my missing vocabulary, with limited snapping required.

I was hoping that my memory would make a recovery as my kid grew, but after talking to parents with older children, I've had to accept that it may have left the building forever. My only hope is for its return after I become an empty-nester and finally have my brain (and my sleep patterns) to myself. The only problem with that plan is that I will be heading into menopause about five minutes later. And that is not a time that is noted for brain function.

So, if you happen to see me on the street in twenty years randomly grabbing people and insisting on having intellectual conversations with them, you'll know why. I'll be in a mad dash to use my vocabulary and brain waves before they disappear once again.

All my MOFLs agreed that their children had also shot their brains to hell. Although a few (show-offs) said that they had eventually recovered.

Salpy hasn't seen her brain for a while. "I can't even remember what my memory was like before I had kids."

Even our Chipper Jen got hit. "It's sooo bad! I still put the gallon of milk in the pantry after pouring it!"

Sarah gives us hope (or makes us feel bad). "My memory definitely was shot, but I feel like everything returned post-baby. But it did take about a year for full recovery."

Sommer, however, is still waiting. "I'm one year in and my most commonly used phrase is 'I'm really sorry, I have a baby and my brain is just mush.' I just wonder how long I can blame it on the baby."

Erika uses some aids, like I do. "I have to write absolutely everything down. I'm very appreciative of the Notes app on my phone, and I set reminders for all kinds of stuff on my calendar. I pretty much never used that stuff before Luke."

Monica agrees. "Yes. Wait, what did you just ask?"

So, if your brain is useless after bringing home a new baby, don't despair. At least you are in good company. Just remember—wait, why am I bothering? You've already forgotten this whole chapter, haven't you?

27

YOUR BODY
IS RUINED

(and your mind is barely hanging on)

Pregnancy (noun)

The glorious time when you are encouraged by society and medical professionals to gain weight. You are considered to be doing well if you are not able to see your own feet or put on your own shoes. "The baby is hungry!" becomes a battle cry and an excuse to eat everything in sight. A time in which exercise can be considered risky and bed rest considered mandatory. The best of times.

The rest of your life (noun)

A time in which a big belly is no longer fawned over with gentle rubs. A time in which exercise is expected, and resting in bed is considered lazy. The most unfortunate of times.

Your body spent forty weeks growing a watermelon, totally re-shaped your various parts to get the watermelon out of you, and then looks nothing like those damn supermodels who are out doing photo shoots a month after their deliveries. Life, as you probably already know, is terribly unkind.

You'll be thinking about how to get your poor body back to its pre-baby glory long before and after your baby arrives. You'll spend months looking down at the body below you and wondering if it will ever reshape back into shape.

Unfortunately and fortunately, I don't have a lot to share in the way of personal experience with this topic. I spent the first twenty weeks of my pregnancy unable to eat more than two bites without gagging, which turned out to be a great weight-loss regimen. I lost fifteen pounds my first two trimesters, and although I came back strong in my last trimester (the perfect combination of a crazy appetite and medical professionals' recommended weight gain), I ended up gaining only about twenty pounds from my starting weight.

By the time I birthed my six-pound baby and what seemed like forty-five pounds of other insides, I was only about ten pounds overweight when I left the hospital. I didn't do much to lose my baby weight, simply because it was very far down on my list of things to give two craps about. I did, however, breastfeed like crazy, and my kid was lactose intolerant, so I didn't eat any dairy for almost a year. It turns out I really enjoy cheese, because cutting it out of my diet resulted in my getting down to below my original weight by the time Vivi was six months old.

The only lingering effect of my pregnancy was the little belly pooch I had that made me constantly look about three months pregnant. Most women would make it their mission to get rid of that pooch. I, however, knew I was going to try to get pregnant again within a couple of years. Why on earth go exerting energy to fix my body when another fetus was going to come along and destroy it again? That just sounds silly. I had cheese to eat.

Not only that, but shortly before we decided to try to get pregnant again, I went on my Dead Man Walking diet. This is the diet of a person whose body is about to be hijacked for the next two years. Between pregnancy and nursing, I knew it would be a long while before I could put anything into my body without knowing that it was affecting my child. There would be no caffeine, a very limited amount of junk food, and no sushi.

Therefore, during my Dead Man Walking diet I was constantly drinking soda, eating fast food, and going kookoo for Kit Kat bars. I gained ten pounds in a month. It was fantastic. I wasn't too worried about this weight gain because my previous experience with pregnancy taught me that it was an excellent way to lose weight.

Fast-forward to my current pregnancy, wherein I once again feel like puking twenty-four hours a day. Unfortunately, there is one slight difference this time. The only way I can keep from getting sick is by eating. Nonstop. So yeah. I'm already starting ten pounds up and I can't stop eating. I see this ending very, very poorly.

My MOFLs have great advice for dealing with my impending post-baby Battle of the Bulge.

Salpy says simply, "Nurse like crazy."

Sarah disagrees on the nursing idea. "Nursing does burn a lot of calories, but it also makes you hungry! Working toward something definitely helps! So running, walking, Insanity Workout DVDs (when you can't leave the house), and the gym."

Chipper Jen shockingly recommends going to the gym. "Be consistent! Find a gym with a good childcare that you trust! Only way I did it! Nursing didn't help me lose any weight right away. My body didn't respond much to workouts right away, either. But eventually it all falls into place if you don't give up!"

Erika recommends going further than just a gym membership. "Pick up a sport or a class that you have to go to at a certain time. This helps you avoid the 'I'll do it later' slump, and it's much more fun than pounding the treadmill."

Michelle, mom of two, skipped the gym and hit the streets. "Walk like crazy! I walked two to three miles daily and lost my weight in three months. No gym membership or babysitter required. The fresh air is good for both Mama and baby, and all you need is a stroller. Keep in mind even if you lose the weight, it may take a while for your hips to shrink down. That took about six months for me."

Sarah gets real. "Accept that every woman's body is different and responds differently to pregnancy and nursing. I trained for and ran marathons after both boys, nursed exclusively, calorie counted, and had a trainer. Still, for whatever reason, it always took my body two years to get back to 'normal' (if that still exists, ha!!)."

Amy thinks you need to shift your idea of normal. "I think a lot of us are never going to look ANYTHING like we did pre-baby without plastic surgery! I'm talking varicose veins, major stretch marks, the 'deflated balloon' skin on the tummy. Things no diet or personal trainer can help in the slightest. So I think it's important in the whole quest to get 'back in shape' to be realistic and to accept that we might need a new definition of 'in shape.'"

Another Amy makes the best point yet. "I decided since the baby came out round and everyone thought she was so cute that I would take on that shape to see if it was cute on me as well. Turns out it isn't as cute on me, but I sure am loving my chocolate chip cookie dough right now."

Mmmm. Cookie dough . . .

PARTNER CORNER: POST-BABY BODY

Larry: I should preface this with the fact that unwanted sexual advances are bad. Now, postpartum it gets cloudy. My advice is to make advances. Better put, make appropriate advances often. Be prepared for the fact that her body may not respond like it used to. She may have developed some new quirks; boob play is no longer fun. She may say no, a lot. She may feel guilty for not wanting to participate as often as before. Be reassuring and verbalize your appreciation for her body and the fact that it gave your family a beautiful baby or two or three. Just make sure she knows that you still want her. You'll be fine.

28

YOU'LL PROBABLY WANT A DIVORCE

(and so will your partner)

Classes they should make expecting couples take instead of silly parenting and birthing classes:

- How to speak to a woman with postpartum depression (first lesson: try not to speak to a woman with postpartum depression)

- Arguing through sign language (get your point across without waking the baby)

- The official rules of roshambo (no, going best three out of five is not an official rule)

- You may never have sex again (and if you do, you'll probably just get pregnant again, so why risk it?)

I don't know if you've sensed my overall theme with this book, but in general, babies are really hard. While they are a wonderful and beautiful addition to your life, they actually systematically destroy that life, one aspect at a time (please see Chapter 12, "Your Life Is Officially Over").

One of the most vulnerable aspects is not talked about very often. That aspect is your relationship. If you are in a relationship before having a child, there is a good chance you will think about getting out of that relationship at some point during the first year you have the child home. But hold off on calling that divorce attorney whose ad you keep seeing on TV in the middle of the night while breastfeeding. No, it is not a sign.

As I mentioned, babies are hard. They'll stress you out, exhaust you, and confuse the hell out of you. And they will do the same to your partner. Unfortunately, because they are so little you can't really take out your frustration on the actual baby (it's illegal). However, if there is another adult nearby, it becomes very easy to redirect that frustration in their direction. It must be *their* fault the baby has been crying for three hours straight!! Finger-pointing activate!!

Two people who were once very rational and kind can be screaming at each other at the top of their lungs within mere hours of bringing a baby home. Or, if the baby is sleeping nearby, through *very* intense exchanges of whispers.

I am very lucky because my partner is a woman. A woman who had previous experience with babies to boot. This meant I had a lot of support and that in reality she was doing most of the heavy lifting. I had no idea what to do with a newborn baby, and besides breastfeeding, I felt pretty useless. My partner, on the other hand, was comfortable around babies and also didn't have intense hormonal issues raging through her body like I did. So she was a little better equipped to deal with the child.

But even with all those pluses in our favor, we still had regular arguments that stemmed mostly from lack of sleep and general frustration in dealing with an inconsolable child. Neither one of us really knew what the answers were, but we were both pretty sure the other one's answers were wrong. I was constantly on the internet trying to figure out the best long-term solutions to our baby issues, while my partner was always more interested in just making the crying stop. Right. This. Second.

One night in particular stands out in our epic battle over whether to let the baby cry it out. Vivian was four months old, but we were still butting heads on the sleep-training issues. I instructed my partner not to pick the baby up from the crib if she was crying, but instead to console her with some soft words and a gentle touch. If we picked the baby up during my attempts to sleep-train her, we would be hitting reset on our efforts and have to start over from the beginning. The internet said so.

On this particular night there had been a lot of crying, and finally my partner couldn't take it anymore. When I went into the baby's room and saw Becky holding the baby, I said, "Fine! If you want to pick her up, then *you* get to deal with her the rest of the night!"

I went back into our dark room and got into bed. Becky came storming in after me. She turned on the light and tapped me on the shoulder. Why? Because I didn't have my hearing aids in and can't hear without them. When I looked up she mouthed the words (so I could read her lips) "I hate you!!" Then she turned off the lights and stormed out of the room.

This is a small glimpse into the life of new parents (and the hearing impaired). My partner doesn't hate me (often). She had just been worn down by the nonstop screaming of her child. She hated that I was done dealing with the baby for the night and that I could actually say that, because I wouldn't be kept awake by the crying (a benefit of hearing impairment).

I honestly can't remember how that night ended, but I can tell you that we were laughing about it the next day. I said, "You come running into the room screaming at me!" To which she replied, "No, I didn't actually say anything, I just mouthed the words."

There can be a lot of reasons couples fight with the addition of a new baby, including stress, financial woes, sleep deprivation, unequal participation by both partners, and disagreements over how to best care for the child. Even the healthiest relationships will feel the strain from bringing a baby home, and sometimes that strain will ebb and flow. Our biggest issues had to do with trying to juggle our work with a new baby (because we were self-employed, we didn't have the standard maternity leave time), general exhaustion, and disagreements on how to tackle different baby issues.

Before a baby comes along, even the closest couples probably don't have much occasion to collaborate on a major project. Most of the time couples go about their day and work, then meet up for dinner and conversation (and by "conversation," I mean TV). Any significant stress is most likely coming from things happening outside the relationship. Then a baby arrives, and all of a sudden the two of you are tasked with managing a very large, very stressful project together. (Also, there is a lot less time for TV.)

Have you ever watched *The Amazing Race*? It's a reality show in which two people who have a preexisting relationship (couples, siblings, parent/child, best friends) race around the world together, completing challenges along the way. The show is entertaining because relationships have a way of changing when exposed to stress. People have a way of changing, too. Sometimes this works out beautifully; sometimes couples break up in Episode 2 following a screaming match in the middle of Budapest.

When you bring a baby home, you and your partner are essentially heading out on your own amazing race. You will be faced with tremendous challenges. You have to navigate new territory and work together in ways that are very new to both of you. If you can get through the race (a.k.a. the baby's first year) without one of you moving to Budapest, you should consider it a resounding success.

Despite the challenges there will also be times when your new one brings the two of you closer together (this will happen mostly when the child is sleeping). If you are both making a constant effort, communicating with each other, and actively participating in baby care, you'll usually end up with a stronger bond once you're past the more difficult parts. Almost like war buddies who have been on the front lines together—if the front lines included way less sand and way more poop.

Knowing that all these challenges are coming your way won't necessarily make them easier to deal with once they appear. But try to set some ground rules in advance to prepare both of you for the upcoming battle. Promise to be kind to each other, even if you want to scream, "I hate you!" Try to always communicate with each other, especially your frustrations and fears. Allow each other a few free passes, in which one of you stays with the baby and the other gets to leave the room for a half hour to regroup. Share the responsibilities that come with a new baby, and don't let one partner skip out simply because he or she may not be as good at certain tasks. In fact, that partner should tackle those tasks early and often, so they can gain confidence. Warn your partner that you will be a hormonal mess (please see Chapter 7, "So Many Tears") and to approach you accordingly. Respect each other's opinions, even if you don't always agree. From the very beginning try to find someone to come over for an hour or two so the both of you can get out of the house together without the baby.

More than anything, remind yourselves that you both have something to bring to your new table. You both love this baby more than anything and are deeply invested in its well-being. There is tremendous value in sharing this journey with someone who cares as much as you do, who is just as scared as you are. This isn't just some friend you are asking for advice; this is your partner whom you've committed to tackling all of life's adventures with. Hell, after all this you guys will be shoo-ins for a spot on *The Amazing Race*. You'll be unstoppable!

I asked my MOFLs for their advice on avoiding divorce during the baby's first year, and this is what they had to share.

Dana says, "This is a big one! I feel like having a baby can bring you closer in so many ways, but it can also have you at each other's throats. I think that's because the first year can be so hard physically, emotionally, and mentally that you just want to feel supported. However, that being said, even if you are being supported by your significant other, it sort of feels like it's never enough at times. It can feel like you are doing everything, and it can be annoying when you realize that your significant other's life hasn't been as dramatically affected by your little one as yours. That can cause some resentment. I think the best piece of advice is to try to communicate with each other as best as possible. Overall, you just need to look at the bigger picture and be thankful for the beautiful baby that you both brought into the world together."

Salpy recommends seeing the positives in your partner. "Try to notice and appreciate everything your husband does to help. Saying thank you goes a lot further than complaining about what he ISN'T doing."

Salpy has a lot better handle on her emotions than most of us, it would seem.

Sommer touches upon another issue that comes up sometimes. "Honestly, my husband became very jealous that my attention was going to Kash rather than to him. This lasted for quite a while. Kash is one year old, and I finally feel that he accepts the situation (not understands or loves, just accepts). It's hard to feel yourself changing, becoming a 'mommy,' and hoping to God your husband is on board to change with you and likes you in your new sense of self."

Even Chipper Jen struggled. "The hardest thing for me was that I wanted to do everything and do it right. I thought I should be able to be 'supermom' and 'superwife'! That's a hard job! And all the changes were really hard on me, emotionally and physically. Since I was breastfeeding, even if we did get a night out, my boobs clearly reminded me that I had a curfew. And at times it was too hard to get the kids settled and get ready to go anywhere. I was exhausted before we even got in the car! So I never wanted to leave them. That was hard for us because my hubby missed having date nights like we did before."

Jenine had a bit of a wake-up call when her kids came along and disrupted her marriage. "This was the hardest part of parenting for me! I felt like I was totally slapped upside the head with the idea that my husband was not the most awesome dude ever! He's just a regular guy, and when deprived of sleep and put under stress, he loses his patience just like everyone else. Seems obvious when put into words, but I really think I mourned the loss of the old husband a lot. Now that we've been in it a few years, we struggle to maintain the fun stuff and not just fall into the business partner rut. Who knew you had to work at it?! So many clichés coming true!"

Monica gives the simplest answer of all. "Politely ask him to move out for a year."

Good point, Monica. I hear Budapest is lovely this time of year.

PARTNER CORNER: DIVORCE?

Pat: It's an insanely difficult time. You will think about divorce a lot. And if you're not thinking about divorce, your partner is. Do yourself a favor and get some therapy. Contact your HR department and ask about the company's employee assistance program. There was so much strain on us that we decided quickly that we did not want another child.

Tom: Take a breath. Don't say the first thing you want to say because it's probably fueled by exhaustion, frustration, and the overwhelming sensation that you're in way over your head. She's feeling the exact same way you are, so if SHE says something you know she didn't mean, realize that, and don't make it an excuse to fire back and start World War III.

Larry: Immediately after the thought of divorce crossed my mind, so did the thought of raising a child by myself. That was enough for me to come back to earth. In the big picture baby stress was such a small part of our relationship.

29

IT DOES NOT GO BY "SOOOO FAST"

(lack of sleep = lack of speed)

2,526,253	**vs.**	**2,526,254**
Number of times friends, strangers, and mostly people who haven't had a baby in over twenty-five years will tell you,		Number of times in the first month of your child's life you will think to yourself (and/or scream out to the heavens),
"Cherish every moment; it all goes by soooo fast."		"Will this ever end????"

Things that make time fly by:

- Fun

- Sleeping for more than three hours at a time (see "Fun" above)

- Vacation

- Booze

Things that make time screech to a puke-covered, sleep-deprived halt:

- Being covered in puke

- Being sleep deprived

- Spending 98.99 percent of your day with something latched to your boob

- Mandatory sobriety

Without fail, and most likely before you even leave the hospital, a woman will approach you with the sage advice/warning "It all goes by so fast!"

Since you will inevitably be holding a newborn at the time, you will be left to assume that "in a blink of an eye" your new baby will be heading off to college (or moving into your basement while he pursues his woodworking passion). It's a scary thought, the baby years zooming by. But it's a thought that becomes increasingly less frightening as your new life starts to unfold.

Late one night you'll tell yourself, "I know that the baby just broke the sound barrier with his screams for two hours straight, and I'm pretty sure that awful smell is coming from my clothes and not the child, but don't worry—this is all going to whiz right by. Just keep blinking—he'll be studying for his SATs in no time!"

But then it doesn't whiz by. It doesn't even sputter. In fact, in a cruel twist of fate, time actually starts standing still. How is this possible? Simple, really. Have you ever stared at a digital clock, waiting for the time to change? Never will sixty seconds pass slower than when you are doing nothing but waiting for sixty seconds to pass. The same is true with newborns. During the most trying days (scream, puke, poop—repeat) all you are doing is staring at that little baby, willing this moment to pass. And cursing the cruelty of every person who told you it was going to fly right by.

One day you'll be out at the supermarket with your child, scouring the baby aisle for answers, when an acquaintance will come up to you and start fawning over the infant. They will ask how old the child is, you will answer, and then they will say, "Already?! Wow, time flies!" You will look at them, nod, and smile, all while thinking to yourself, *So I've heard.* Then you will try to discreetly head over to the snack aisle.

You'll bury your nose in books and websites, searching for answers as to when the "fast" part starts. You'll start texting other mothers you know, forcing them to repeatedly tell you it will get better, demanding that they give you a specific date. You grasp onto every little milestone the child has ("That was a smile!" "No, that was gas." "I'll take it!"), hoping that it's edging you closer to the child eventually being something other than a crying, pooping, eating blob of baby.

If you need further help in grasping the simple fact that time will not go by quickly, I've prepared a simple equation for you:

Baby + Screaming – Sleep = Time Screeching to a Halt

Now, to be fair, *any* equation that involves the subtraction of precious sleep will pretty much always result in time halting. But it takes the unique vocal capacity of a baby to really make it screech.

If there is a silver lining to your winter (and spring and summer and fall) of discontent, it has to be the fact that every parent on the planet eventually ends up uttering the words "It all goes by so fast." Every parent has been where you are, and yet they all eventually got to a point where the baby days felt really fast in retrospect. Just because you haven't gotten to the retrospect *yet* doesn't mean you, too, won't someday verbally assault some haggard new mother with warnings of flying time.

Twenty years ago I was in high school. I'm proud of where I've gotten in these past two decades and how I got here, but when I see high school kids today, I'm secretly jealous of all that still lies before them:

the possibilities they will get to explore in their twenties and thirties. It's not that I regret missing out on any possibilities myself, because Lord knows I explored; it's that I envy the feeling of just starting out on life's adventures. I want to take each graduating senior aside and impart the knowledge I've gained. I want to tell them not to be scared of the unknown, to not ever let the world or their own thoughts limit their potential. I want to instruct them to maximize every second of their youth and freedom, because in retrospect I see that those were my most fleeting resources. But who can talk to teenagers, really?

I think the same goes for older parents who spot newborns and new parents. They flash back to when their children were clean slates (long before they moved into the basement with all that wood), and they envy that you are just starting out on your new life adventure. Time quickly moves in reverse, from today, back through proms, driver's permits, braces, dance recitals, soccer games, sleepovers, tooth fairies, Christmas mornings, first steps, first giggles, first breaths. They want to tell you that all the moments, even the difficult ones, add up to something great. They see the dark circles under your eyes and that you are barely hanging on to a squirming infant, but they want you to know it's worth it. It's all so worth it. They want you to maximize every second of your child's youth—because in retrospect they see how fleeting it all was. But who can talk to new parents, really?

Instead all they say is "It all goes by so fast." And they hope those words will hit you as a warning, but instead we tend to take them as a promise.

So in twenty years, when you spot a new mother, instead of lying to the poor woman, simply say, "I know it's really, really hard right now, a lot harder than anyone warned you about. But eventually they will sleep, I promise, and someday they will personally take care of all matters regarding their own poop. And for as hard as it all is and will be, your heart will actually break in two when they grow up and move out of your house one day. Your time spent with that squirmy little blob will become the greatest privilege of your life. I promise."

Then head to the snack aisle with pride, because Lord knows you've earned it.

PARTNER CORNER: THE BABY TIME WARP

Jason: I hated when people told me how fast it went . . . the first six months were almost certainly the longest of my life. So . . . now in retrospect it looks short, but then, those days were four hundred hours long and sometimes miserable.

I still tell my guy friends with new babies: The first six months suck. The baby shits and sleeps and steals the boobs. But then, it starts to get a little interesting. And by a year, things are a hundred times easier, and your "creature" went from basically an animal to a real-life human. And it only keeps getting better and better.

Larry: Simply, it can't last forever. The good news is that the human brain is good at tossing out traumatic experiences. So . . .

EPILOGUE

A s you've seen in the chapters of this book, the first year with a baby can be challenging, to say the least. Your world gets turned upside down, and the new life you are left holding is messy, confusing, and requires a lot more laundry than you are used to. (You know you are in for a wild ride when navigating a watermelon out of your uterus is the least traumatizing part of this whole experience.)

Now that my daughter is eighteen months old and I have another baby on the way, I wonder whether I'll take the things I learned last time and use them to make my next round a little easier. I often think about the advice I will give myself when Baby Dos arrives. The things I wish I had done last time.

While I don't think any experience or magic advice will suddenly make the first year with the new baby easy, I do think I'll approach the experience a little differently the next time. The biggest reason I freaked the hell out when I was told I would not be getting drugs during childbirth was because I had no idea how long it was going to last. I had heard of people pushing for hours and hours. The thought of enduring that pain for hours and hours overloaded my brain and flipped the crazy switch. Had I known I was only in for another forty minutes of pain, the fear of the unknown would have subsided. (No guarantee that the f-bombs would have stopped, though.)

Most of the first year with Vivian was a lot like her birth. When things were difficult they seemed endless. I had no frame of reference for how long every stage was going to last, so I just automatically assumed it would be difficult forever. I know that is not logical, but at the time that's how it felt.

As a result I was always in a rush to get to the next stage. I couldn't wait for her to smile, then roll over, then sit up, then crawl, then wean, then walk, then go to college and get a good stable job with a 401(k)—you know, all the milestones. To me, each of those milestones meant that we were moving closer to the biggest milestone of all: "when Mommy stops feeling so damned overwhelmed."

Eventually I realized that Mommy is never going to stop feeling overwhelmed, as long as Mommy is doing her job right. And all I really ended up doing was neglecting the current stage because I was always looking ahead for the next one.

Now that I know what is in store for us with a newborn, I hope I can slow down a bit with Baby Dos (although battling Vivian's terrible twos at the same time will be an entirely new adventure that I probably won't mind trying to fast-forward a bit). Beyond keeping an eye out for alarming development delays, I don't think I'll care so much when he hits the required milestones. I've realized all kids get there eventually, and when they do they all start moving away from their parents a lot faster, so why rush it?

I also hope I'm a bit gentler with myself this next go-around. I'm a perfectionist at heart, and parenting is most definitely not for perfectionists. It has a way of making you feel very, very imperfect most of the time. Over the past year and a half, I've had to shift my expectations a little bit—of myself, my family, my house, and my child. We are far from perfect, but we are happy. Even if sometimes the dishes are piled too high, Vivian's hair is a little too messy, and the circles under her mommies' eyes are a little too dark. Every day there is laughter in her home, and every day she knows how much she is loved. I've learned to relax a bit and realize that those things make up a pretty damn good day just by themselves.

There is an Anne Rice quote I read long before I had a child, but one I always knew represented what I wanted to give my children someday: "He moved with a grace and dignity that only comes from having once been cherished."

Cherish your children, and cherish who you are with them. Feel free to admire exactly how much ass you have to kick between breakfast time and bath time to keep these kids cherished. And never feel like you are alone out there. You are a MOFL, one of the many battling every day to keep your kids safe and yourself sane.

Be kind to yourselves and one another when you meet up along the way. Let that mom who is losing to a screaming child in the supermarket know that you've been there. Give the woman trying to change a squirming poopy child in a public restroom a gentle smile. Ask your mom friends how they are doing, and provide judgment-free support.

We are all in this together. We are the many. The tired. The Moms.

See you out on the front lines, ladies.

ACKNOWLEDGMENTS

To my agents, Lilly Ghahremani and Stefanie Von Borstel, who have always worked so hard for me, but who worked especially hard this time to guarantee my book would have the word "Sh!t" in the title. Dreams come true, kids. To my editor, Brooke Warner, for believing in my voice since my first book and encouraging it along the way.

To my Moms on the Front Lines (Chipper Jen, Dana, Carrie, Karen, Michelle, Amy C., Melanie, Sarah B., Amy S., Jenine, Erika, Sarah G., Jodi, Sommer, Salpy, Jill, Monica, Brooke, Channing, and Viki) for playing along with my ridiculous and sometimes very personal questions. Their honesty and humor contributed so much to this book, and it's been great fun getting to know all of them better through this process of oversharing.

To Chipper Jen Cate in particular for always being just a text message away when I doubted any and all things parenting and baby (there have been a lot of text messages). Her quick and helpful advice has calmed me down countless times and probably stopped at least twenty-seven panic-induced emergency room visits.

To Jodi Holmes, who has been my best friend since second grade (we won't go on record about how many years that has been). It is so much fun to watch our two little girls become friends as well.

Although, karma may have some interesting things in mind for us when they are in their teens ...

To Michelle Roloff, for loving and watching over our daughter the first year of her life. And for teaching her how to shop with purpose.

To all the people who have chipped in to help in this crazy kid/life/work balancing act: Rose Marie Garofalo, Andrea LaMattina, and countless others.

To my dad, Dave Dais, for falling head over heels in love with his first grandchild and for documenting pretty much every second of her existence with a photo. To my mom, Betty Lou Dais, for teaching me how to be a good mother and showing Vivian every day what it's like to have an amazing grandmother.

To Becky Rook. She grabbed onto little Vivian's hands as soon as she came out and hasn't stopped protecting her ever since.

To my little Vivi bean, bringing you into this world and watching you make your way through it has been the biggest joy of my life. For your giggles, your hugs, and your kindness. And for being able to sit through an entire two-hour Disney movie when Mommy needs to lie on the couch for a little while.

Thank you.

Dawn Dais is the author of six other guides to pregnancy and parenting, including *The Sh!t No One Tells You About Pregnancy* and *The Sh!t No One Tells You About Toddlers*. She lives in Roseville, California, with her two children, Vivian and Daniel. She is tired.

Stalk Dawn online at www.dawndais.com.

BACKCOUNTRY HUTS & LODGES
of the
ROCKIES & COLUMBIAS

The Alpine Club of Canada is pleased to
endorse this comprehensive guide to the
many backcountry huts and lodges in the
Rocky and Columbia mountain ranges.